Contents

THE
MUTE SWAN

Mike Birkhead and Christopher Perrins

CROOM HELM
London

© 1986 Mike Birkhead and Christopher Perrins
Photographs by Mike Birkhead and Christopher Perrins
Line drawings by David Quinn
Croom Helm Ltd, Provident House, Burrell Row, Beckenham,
Kent, BR3 1AT

British Library Cataloguing in Publication Data

Birkhead, Mike
    The mute swan.
    1. Swans
    I. Title   II. Perrins, Christopher
    598.4'1 QL696.A52

    ISBN 0-7099-3259-6

Typeset in ITC Garamond Light
by Leaper & Gard Ltd, Bristol
Printed and bound in Great Britain
by Biddles Ltd, Guildford and Kings Lynn

Black-and-white Plates

Line-drawings

Preface

Few people, however little their interest in birds, would deny that the Mute Swan is one of the finest sights in the English countryside. A pair of these large, white birds patrolling their breeding territory in winter or the same pair in summer with a brood of downy, grey cygnets provides the 'high-spot' on many a country walk. Their large size and, in many areas, their approachability mean that one does not have to have binoculars or telescope to be able to watch them easily.

As a result, Mute Swans have been an accepted part of the British countryside for so long that most people do not think twice about them. They are so conspicuous that, for a long time, even ornithologists tended to ignore them. Indeed, in the early 1960s, very little was known of the details of their breeding biology and life-history — far less than was known, for example, about most of our common woodland birds such as the Robin, Blue Tit or Blackbird.

This rather odd situation started to change in the early 1960s when it was realised that the Mute Swan was a good bird for study, especially for looking at certain aspects of life-history and population biology. To take but one example, most ornithologists looking at bird populations find it difficult to discover what proportion of the population does not breed, or indeed whether there is a non-breeding population at all! Birds that do not take up a territory, but move around the countryside, are exceedingly difficult to count or even to find. At least with a bird the size of a swan, there is a reasonably good chance of finding and counting all the individuals in a given area.

It was fortuitous that some of these studies started when they did, for, although it was not realised at the time, major changes were afoot in the

Mute Swan populations, especially among those on the lowland English rivers. In many areas, their numbers were starting to decline markedly. Without some of this early information on numbers and survival rates, it would have been more difficult to assess what was happening. We discuss what is known about the population changes and the reasons for them in later chapters, together with the outlook for the future of the swans on these rivers (Chapter 8).

Acknowledgements

Few people can write a book on birds in isolation. In the case of the Mute Swan this would be quite impossible and, as a result, we owe more thanks than most.

First and foremost, the Mute Swan is a Royal Bird and those which live on the lower reaches of the Thames are still claimed by the Lord Chamberlain's Office (on behalf of the Crown) and the two livery companies, the Worshipful Company of Vintners and the Worshipful Company of Dyers. The former company received rights to the swans in 1472 or shortly afterwards, probably through David Selby, who was Master of the Vintners Company in 1439-40 and owned rights to swans himself; the Dyers obtained their rights shortly after the Vintners, sometime before 1483. It is these bodies who maintain the annual tradition of catching up (or 'upping') the swans and marking them. In late July, they catch all the breeding swans and their broods on the Thames during the colourful ceremony of 'swan-upping'. It was these bodies, too, who first became concerned about the declining numbers of swans on the river. Because of the studies we had made on the swans around Oxford, they asked us to extend our studies downstream and to look into the reasons for the decline. We are most grateful to them for their assistance and for allowing us to look at old records in their care. In addition, we have been greatly helped by Mr John Turk, Her Majesty's Swan Keeper, and by the Barge Masters of the two companies, Mr Bill Colley of the Vintners and Mr Harold Cobb of the Dyers.

We discuss briefly the swans at Abbotsbury, Dorset, and their history. These too are privately owned, and we are grateful to the owner, Lady Teresa Agnew, for allowing one of us (CMP) and Dr Malcolm Ogilvie of the Wildfowl Trust to study them. We are also especially grateful to the warden of the Swannery, Mr John Fair, for his continued help and interest.

We have also been allowed access to the findings of other people studying swans. The main studies are mentioned below, and here again we are most grateful to these workers for their generosity and help. In addition, we have had veterinary help and advice from Francis Clegg and Alan Hunt of the Ministry of Agriculture, Fisheries and Food; they have been responsible for most of the analyses of dead birds and of blood samples taken during our investigations. Similarly, Mike French of the Institute of Terrestrial Ecology, who has been making parallel studies in East Anglia, has been most helpful to us. Mr and Mrs Steve Cooke have taken into care many sick swans on the Thames and have kindly helped us with advice and information.

In order to get access to the swans, we have usually needed to go on to private land and have almost invariably been allowed to do so. For much of our inquiry into the decline along the Thames, we have been dependent on members of the public providing us with information and reporting dead swans to us. Without their continued help, much of the study would have been impossible. We hope that some recent changes, discussed more fully in Chapter 8, will herald a somewhat rosier future for the swans. These changes have been brought about, in some measure at least, because of the information provided by our studies. We hope that all who have made it possible for us to provide this information will feel that their efforts were worthwhile.

We are also grateful to the following for commenting on various drafts of the text: Dr L. Batten, Dr T.R. Birkhead, Dr A.S. Cooke, I. McPhail, Dr M.A. Ogilvie, Dr D.K. Scott, Miss E.J. Sears and Dr G. Thomas. Caroline Aitzetmuller kindly typed parts of the text. In addition we would like to thank David Quinn for his lovely line drawings.

Some of the recent studies into the reasons for the decline of Mute Swans on the River Thames have been funded by a number of organisations, including: the Lord Chamberlain's Office, the Vintners and the Dyers Companies, the Nature Conservancy Council, the Royal Society for the Protection of Birds, the International Fund for Animal Welfare, the Ernest Cooke Trust, the World Wildlife Fund, and the Water Research Centre.

Finally, we would like to thank David Christie who did an incredibly thorough and laborious job in editing the text so well. To him many thanks.

The Main Studies of Swans

A number of studies of the Mute Swan started up in the 1960s and in the 1970s, so that today it is one of our better-known species. Much, however, remains to be found out about regional variations in the swan's biology, for, as we shall show, there are marked differences between the regions so far studied. The major studies which have been carried out are:

(1) In the English Midlands, by A.E. Coleman and Dr C.D.T. Minton.

(2) On the Upper Thames and its tributaries, later extended to the Lower Thames as well, by ourselves together with a number of co-workers, especially C.M. Reynolds, Dr P.E. Bacon and Miss J.E. Sears.

(3) On the colony of swans that breed at Abbotsbury on the Fleet in Dorset, by one of us (CMP) and by Dr M.A. Ogilvie of the Wildfowl Trust.

These long-term studies were augmented by several others, including a valuable, though shorter, one of the Mute Swans in the Hebrides by Professor G.M. Dunnet and Dr C.J. Spray from Aberdeen University. In addition, a number of amateur groups have made local studies in other areas and, by ringing large numbers of swans, have added greatly to our knowledge of the movements and survival of the Mute Swan.

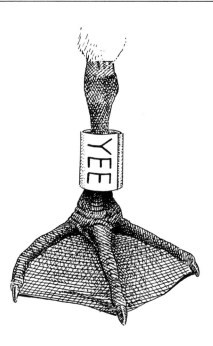

Many Mute Swans, especially in the south of England, have unique 'Darvic' identification rings on their legs

Our aim has been to make this a serious, but, we hope, a readable account of the Mute Swan in Britain. As such, we have not weighed down the text with statistics. Equally, we have tried to avoid citing too many references. We have tried to provide the sources of the information that we present for the serious reader, but, in order to minimise the number of references in the text, we have usually omitted references to any of the main studies mentioned above. Readers wishing to find the source of such information should be able to locate it by referring to the names given above in the Bibliography. For example, information about the swans in the Midlands is mostly to be found in the papers by Coleman or Minton.

Plate 1. A magnificent male Mute Swan 'shakes down' after a preening session

Introduction

Classification of Wildfowl

Although in this book we are really concerned only with the commonest British species of swan, the Mute Swan, *Cygnus olor*, it seems worthwhile briefly to put this species into context by saying something about its relatives, especially since the other European swans sometimes cause confusion.

Swans belong to the Order of birds known as Anseriformes, an order including almost 150 species — the ducks, geese and swans. This group is among the most important of all birds to man; not only are many valuable in sport, but the Mallard, *Anas platyrhynchos*, is the ancestor of the domestic duck and the Greylag Goose, *Anser anser*, the ancestor of most varieties of domestic geese.

Wildfowl are fairly large, as birds go. The smallest species of teal and pygmy geese weigh only about 250 g, but most are considerably larger than this. The biggest are the swans, some of which are among the largest of all flying birds. Males of three species, Trumpeter, Whooper and Mute, may occasionally tip the scales at 16 kg (about 33 lb). There are even heavier individuals on record, including a Mute of 22.5 kg. Records of birds as large as this are pretty suspect, and they may refer to exaggerated claims of hunters or to obese birds in zoos; we doubt that a swan of 22.5 kg would be able to take off!

The males of many species of wildfowl are conspicuously coloured, whereas the females have fairly dull coloration; the females do all the incubation and so they need to be well camouflaged when on the nest. The geese and swans do not conform to this, the sexes being similar in appearance in most species of geese and in all swans. In the case of the white swans, the birds may be conspicuous on their nests — though they usually nest in fairly inaccessible places, often on small islands if these are available, or tucked away in reedbeds.

As a group, wildfowl are largely aquatic birds; not surprisingly, almost all species have webbed feet and can swim well. Most wildfowl are vege-tarians, though some of the ducks feed on insects, snails and mussels, and a few feed mainly on fish. All the geese and swans are primarily vegetarians. Many of the geese are grazing species and are not so dependent on water as are the ducks.

Wildfowl lay relatively large numbers of eggs compared with many other birds of similar size. The young birds, as soon as they hatch and their down has dried, leave the nest; most can run and swim strongly within about 24 hours of hatching.

While caring for their growing — and still flightless — young, the parents moult. During this moult, the adults of most species drop all their flight feathers simultaneously, becoming flightless themselves. This feature of their annual cycle plays a crucial part in our story of the history of the Mute Swan in Britain, for, by becoming flightless, the birds could be — relatively — easily caught.

The Species of Swans

A good general description of all the species of swans is given in Scott *et al.* (1972). There is a slight complication about how many species of swans there are, since we use eight English names for what scientists regard as seven species! This problem is discussed further under the two birds concerned, the Bewick's and Whistling Swans. For simplicity, we list all eight birds below, but it should be remembered that most orni-thologists regard the Bewick's and Whistling Swans as subspecies of the same species.

The Coscoroba Swan, *Coscoroba coscoroba*. This is an all-white bird from southern South America. It is a shorter-necked species than any of the other swans, and it differs in a number of other respects as well. Indeed, the closeness of its relationship to the other species has been disputed, and it may not be a true swan at all. At present it is treated as a rather aberrant species of swan, the only member of the Genus *Coscoroba*; all other swans are put in the Genus *Cygnus*.

The Black-necked Swan, *Cygnus melanocoryphus*. This is another South American species, a dainty, white bird with, as its name suggests, a black neck and head, the black broken only by a thin white line that runs from the top of the beak, through the eye and around to the back of the head. The bill is bluish-grey, becoming pinkish at the base, and there is a bright red knob at the base of the bill.

The Black Swan, *Cygnus atratus*, is the only Australian species of swan. It is a dark, greyish-black bird except for white flight feathers, which are conspicuous only when it is in flight. This species is quite commonly kept on private waters and may be seen as an escape in

Europe. For most of the early half of this century, there was a feral population of Black Swans on the River Thames. These were owned by the Vintners Company. The records are incomplete, but the highest number seems to have occurred in 1904, when there were 39 Black Swans at 'swan-upping' (see Chapter 2). It is not recorded how many of these were cygnets, but the birds apparently bred successfully for some time. Cygnets were recorded every year during the 1930s and the early 1940s, with as many as nine cygnets in 1931 and seven in 1930 and 1932; the population dwindled during World War Two and seems to have died out shortly afterwards.

The Mute Swan, *Cygnus olor*, the subject of this book.

All the species mentioned so far have reddish bills. The remaining ones have yellow and black, or almost wholly black, beaks and the adult plumage of all four is completely white. It is these four birds which give rise to the problem of how many species there are. Today, two of them, the Trumpeter and the Whistling Swans, occur naturally in North America; the other two, the Whooper and the Bewick's Swans, are found in the Old World. The Trumpeter and Whooper are quite similar to each other, as are the Whistling and Bewick's Swans. Almost certainly, each 'pair' of swans has evolved from a common ancestor which was once found in both the Old and the New Worlds. Probably, during one of the Ice Ages, each of these ancestors became split into two separate populations for a considerable time, so that they developed differences (this is a common way in which speciation in birds is thought to have taken place). Today, the scientist looking at the birds has to decide whether or not the two populations of descendants are still sufficiently similar to be grouped as subspecies of a single species, or whether they have evolved sufficient differences to be ranked as separate species. In these two par-

The three species of swan that are found in Britain. The Mute Swan (a) is present all year round; the Bewick's (b) and Whooper (c) Swans are only winter visitors

ticular cases, the Trumpeter and Whooper have been judged to have diverged sufficiently to be considered separate species, while the Whistling and Bewick's have not yet achieved sufficient differences and so are thought to be best treated as subspecies of the same species. Hence the rather inconvenient situation which we described above: bird-watchers use eight different English names for what scientists regard as seven species of swans.

The Whistling Swan, *Cygnus columbianus columbianus*. This bird is common in parts of North America, breeding in the far north and spending the winter in marshes and estuaries to the south. It has a largely black beak, as opposed to the Old World subspecies' yellow and black one.

The Bewick's Swan, *Cygnus columbianus bewickii*, is the Eurasian counterpart of the Whistling Swan. It breeds in northern Russia and migrates south to warmer areas for the winter. Some 5,000-5,500 come to Britain during the winter; in particular, large numbers have taken to spending this period of the year on parts of the Ouse Washes in Cambridgeshire and Norfolk, where as many as 5,000 have been recorded. It has a yellow and black beak, the patterning being slightly different on each bird which enables the individuals to be told apart.

The Trumpeter Swan, *Cygnus buccinator*, is another North American species. It is, perhaps, just the largest of all swans. It has a black beak. It breeds in northern USA and Canada and is currently the rarest of the species. It must once have been plentiful, but it was heavily hunted. In the period from 1823 to 1880, the Hudson Bay Company sold 108,000 swan skins, largely Trumpeters, in London. In addition, an unknown but probably very large number were killed and sold elsewhere. Such a heavy hunting pressure must surely have been responsible for the scarcity of the species in the early part of this century. By 1932 it was reduced to 69 birds, mostly in Yellowstone National Park, plus some in Canada. Strict protection helped it to recover: by 1960 there were approaching 2,000 individuals, and the build-up in numbers has continued since then, reaching some 10,000 birds in the early 1980s (Harwood 1982).

The Whooper Swan, *Cygnus cygnus*, is the Eurasian equivalent of the Trumpeter Swan. Like the Bewick's Swan, it migrates to northern breeding grounds in summer (though not so far north as the Bewick's); a few pairs have bred in Scotland in some years. Some 2,000-2,500 birds spend the winter in Britain.

The Mute Swan

The Mute Swan was given the scientific name *Cygnus olor*, two words both meaning 'swan', the former being the Latin and the latter apparently derived from an old Celtic name for the bird (Macleod 1954). 'Mute' is a fairly recent name for this species. Until about 1830, people did not distinguish the two yellow-billed swans, Whooper and Bewick's, as separate species (Yarrell 1838). To them, there were only two sorts of swans and, since virtually all Mute Swans were pinioned and in captivity, they called the two types 'Wild' and 'Tame' Swans. The Whooper and Bewick's are still sometimes referred to as 'Wild Swans'. The English naturalist Pennant originally gave the name of Tame Swan to the Mute in 1768. Later, however, he learned that these birds bred wild in Russia, and in 1785 coined the name 'Mute' for them in contrast to the noisy Whooper.

Calls

Mute was an odd name to choose, for silent it is certainly not. The Mute Swan has a series of clearly audible calls, in particular a range of rather quiet honk-like notes and snorts. In addition, it makes a loud hissing when threatened (the Russian name for the Mute Swan, ШИПУН, means 'hissing'). The young have a quite loud and high-pitched piping call, retained even up to and after the time when they are full-grown, at which stage the peeping noise sounds rather pathetic for such large birds. A number of quiet noises are also made during courtship (Boase 1959, Cross 1947, Huxley 1947).

It is true that, in comparison with several of the other species of swans, the Mute Swan's voice is muted. The Trumpeter, Whooper and Whistling Swans have not acquired their names by chance; all have distinctive, far-carrying calls. They are able to give these powerful calls because of their long, complex tracheae (windpipes). These differ in the length and extent of the convolutions, and this is thought to be the reason for the different calls in the different species. The tracheae of the Whooper and Trumpeter Swans are particularly long and complex, with a loop which penetrates the keel (sternum). In contrast, the trachea of the Mute Swan is simpler and the keel lacks the cavity found in the other species (Yarrell 1845, Heinroth and Heinroth 1928).

The whistling or singing note heard when Mute Swans are in flight is made by the wings. As the other British swans do not make this noise in flight, it is a useful way of recognising the Mute Swan as it flies over, especially in the dark. Indeed, it has been suggested that the noise is an adaptation to help the birds to keep in contact with each other in flight, and possibly also to help reduce the chance of mid-air collisions in the dark when several birds are flying together. It may, therefore, be an important contact note between the birds. If this is really so, one wonders why the other swans do not make a similar noise. The answer to this would seem to be that they are much more vocal in flight; the Mute Swan has developed a wing noise for contact purposes, while the other species use their voice. Lockwood (1984) has even suggested that the origin of the word swan can be traced back to the Sanskrit *svanos*, meaning sound, and that this is probably associated not with any of the calls, but with the distinctive sound of the wings of the Mute Swan.

General Appearance

We hesitate to describe the appearance of the Mute Swan, since presumably anybody interested enough to open this book is well aware of what the bird looks like! The cygnets, when they first hatch, are a pale grey above, with white underparts. After a few weeks, the first true feathers start to grow through and these are a greyish-brown. As the birds continue to grow, the 'ugly-duckling' stage is reached, when the bird is a mixture of patches of down and dull brown feathers. The young become more or less fully grown by about September (they do grow a little more during the first year or so); by then they look fairly respectable, but are still largely brown, though with quite a lot of white on the large flight feathers. Their bills are a dark, leaden grey; historically, these young birds were sometimes called blue-bills.

During their first winter, the young birds gradually moult, shedding most of their brown body feathers and replacing these with white ones. This is a fairly continuous process, the plumage becoming progressively whiter with time. None of these young swans, however, becomes fully white until the following summer, when they are just over 12 months old. Throughout this time they can be easily recognised as first-year birds, since they never lose all their brown feathers; at the least they retain a few small brown feathers on the lower back. In addition, their bills remain grey for most of this time.

During their second year, the immature swans become similar in appearance to the fully adult birds. The only thing that usually distinguishes them from older birds (and even this is not wholly reliable as the year progresses) is that the bill colour, which by now has become orange, does not attain the rich reddish-orange of the adults for another year or more. By the time that the young are two years old, most are indistinguishable from adults, and indeed there are occasional records of birds breeding when only two years of age.

Once the fully white plumage is achieved, the swans stay white for the rest of their lives. They do this by an annual moult in July and August. Because they are flightless at this time (page 103), many of them move to safe places to moult. The moult is a major undertaking for any bird. So far as we know, nobody has ever counted the feathers on a Mute Swan, but people once counted those on a Whistling Swan (Amman 1937). This latter bird, which weighed 6.1 kg, had 25,216 feathers weighing 621 g, one-tenth of its total weight. Presumably Mute Swans, some of which are twice the weight of this bird, have even more feathers.

Occasionally one sees Mute Swans with a brownish or reddish tinge to the top of the head and the upper neck. This is not a coloration of the feathers, but rather seems to be some kind of staining which arises from the birds' feeding in iron-rich waters.

The Sexes

The sexes of mated pairs can usually be distinguished in the field (they can be sexed by cloacal examination). It is often possible to distinguish males from females by the appearance of their heads. The females not only have smaller heads, but ones that look slightly more domed than those of the males, whose foreheads run down into the slope of the top of the beak without as much of an angle as is usually visible on the female. The black, fleshy knob at the base of the bill is not a reliable indicator of sex, though it is usually more developed in the male than in the female. Females are usually smaller than the males, and this, too, can often be clear in the field; breeding females weigh about 9.5 kg, while their mates weigh about 12 kg (exceptional males may weigh about 15-16 kg, but weights much above this for wild males are very unusual indeed).

A more subtle way of telling the sexes apart can be used in mid-summer for breeding pairs. The parents moult while their cygnets are still unable to fly. Normally, the female loses her flight feathers first. The male loses his only when the female's wing feathers are again well grown. Since the birds use their wings vigorously in defence, this pattern means that one or other of the pair is in a position to defend the brood should it become necessary.

Cob and Pen

The two sexes are usually referred to as the cob (male) and the pen (female). The origin of these names is obscure. They are mentioned in the ancient Swan Laws (page 27), so have obviously been in use for a very long time. It has been suggested that they were used originally to describe the sexes only during the breeding season and not at other times of the year. This may be wrong, since it is easiest to sex swans when they are paired during the breeding season and it may merely be that only breeding-season records have survived.

Although the origins of the words are obscure, Harting (1895) gives an explanation for them. According to him, cob is derived from the Anglo-Saxon *copp* (the German equivalent is *Kopf*), a word meaning 'top', as in the word 'coping-stone'. In the swan, according to Harting, this refers to the large knob at the base of the bill on the male. Harting further explains that pen is derived from *penne*, meaning feather. This is an odd suggestion, since both sexes have feathers. Harting says, how-ever, not very convincingly, that this refers to the female's habit of swimming along in front of the brood with her wings partially raised and the large flight feathers conspicuous. Harting's views were supported by Ticehurst (1895).

The male Mute Swan (b) is often distinguishable from the female (a) by the larger black knob of tissue at the top of its bill

'Polish Swans'

There is a colour form of the Mute Swan in which the cygnets hatch from the egg covered in a pure white down, instead of the usual grey. These young birds have the normal succession of moults, but all their juvenile plumages are white, not brown. In addition to the white plumage, they have pale, slightly pinkish legs, by which birds of this colour variety can be recognised throughout their lives.

The first British specimens of this form were recorded from Staffordshire in 1686 by the English naturalist Plot (1686). For some time after this, the understanding of what a species was and the ways in which species should be named was still in its infancy. Yarrell (1838) thought that these birds must be of a different species from the normal Mute Swan and named them *Cygnus immutabilis* (= unchanging), in recognition that their plumage remained white throughout their lives.

Nowadays, this form is usually referred to as the 'Polish Swan'. The name seems to have been given to it by London poulterers who imported birds from the Baltic. These swans are commoner in eastern Europe than they are in the west; the name 'Polish' is, however, something of a misnomer, since the form is no commoner in Poland than in several other areas of eastern Europe. In some parts of eastern Europe it may make up about 20 per cent of the population, whereas in Britain it is exceedingly rare. One exception to this gradual change as one travels westwards across Europe is the Netherlands, where the Polish Swan is quite common in some areas. It has been suggested that this is because, in the last century, there were quite a number of people who bred swans in the Netherlands and that they selected in favour of the white cygnets because they were more attractive and hence more valuable.

Mute Swans have been introduced to North America, where they are now quite common in parts of New England. They were imported in small numbers into private parks, where they bred and from where many unpinioned young dispersed. There were two particularly large importations which must have contributed substantially to the founding of the American population: 216 were taken in a single shipment in 1910 and 328 in another in 1912 (Phillips 1928). We have been unable to discover from where these birds were imported. The current American stock, however, has quite a high proportion of Polish birds (some 15 per cent), suggesting that the stock originated from eastern Europe, or perhaps from Dutch breeders, rather than from England. Bacon (1980b) has suggested, however, that the Polish form is at its most successful in populations which are at low density or expanding rapidly, as the American population has been; hence it would be valuable to have past records of the percentage of Polish swans in this population.

The genetic basis of the two colour forms has been worked out (Munro *et al.* 1968). There seems to be a single gene which determines whether the cygnets are white or grey. The Polish gene is recessive to the grey form. (Normally there are two genes for each characteristic, one on each of a matching pair of chromosomes. Saying that a gene is recessive means, in this case, that, if the bird has one Polish gene, but the gene on the matching chromosome is for the grey form, the white coloration is 'overruled' by the grey and the cygnet has the normal grey coloration.) Actually the situation is more complex than this simple description, because the genes for these two colour forms occur on the sex chromosomes. The sex chromosomes differ from all the others in that there is a matching pair in one of the sexes (in birds, the male), but only a single chromosome in the other sex (the female). Consequently, a female with the Polish gene is always white (because she has only the one gene, so there can be no second, grey, gene to overrule it), whereas a male cygnet is white only if both genes are for the Polish colour form; two grey genes or one grey and one Polish result in grey cygnets. As a result, many more of the females (26 per cent) are of the Polish form than are the males (10 per cent).

A large male Mute Swan can normally deter most would-be predators

Aggressiveness

Among the many legends about the Mute Swan is the one claiming that it is very aggressive and can break a man's arm or leg. Mute Swans are normally peaceful and unaggressive, but when they have eggs or young they may courageously defend them. Sometimes the cob may extend his defence to a wide area around his family and attack passers-by or even boats. One pair even saw fit to attack persistently a bullock which they saw as a threat (Patrick 1935). Widowed cobs may also sometimes be aggressive for longish periods. Hunt (1815) perhaps summed it all up quite well (the latter part of the statement being a quote from Buffon):

> 'The habits of the Swan are extremely peaceful, except in the defence of the female, or her young, or when a rival intrudes on the possession of his mistress. He then forgets his mildness, becomes ferocious and fights with an obstinate rancour; and a whole day is often insufficient to terminate the quarrel.'

For the most part swans are certainly inoffensive, but there are occasions, especially during the nesting period, when the cob seems to need to clear a wide space around himself and his mate of all potential threats. At this time, he will attack most things, including smaller and quite harmless inhabitants of the river such as ducks and their broods. Certainly this behaviour does their public image little good! We do not know why they behave in this way, although the removal of other waterfowl from the vicinity of their brood just might reduce the chance of disease in the area.

Human beings are in little danger physically from the swan's aggression — though some people seem quite unconvinced of this! Swans can do little harm with their bills, which can only nibble, nor can they usually use their feet in attack. Their main weapon is the wing and they strike with the carpal joint, the joint which is the equivalent of the human wrist. The bony knob on the joint can be a powerful weapon, and the swans can use it to good effect. Nonetheless, it is a great exaggeration to regard them as potentially dangerous. A blow can hurt, but one would have to be very unfortunate to suffer a broken bone. We know of one record of a broken arm (Harting 1896) and this occurred when a hunter tried to retrieve a swan, in its death-throes, which he had shot. In Britain, a person kneeling on the ground ringing cygnets received a couple of cracked ribs from the irate cob. In both these cases the attacks, from the swan's point of view, were entirely understandable. Persons behaving normally are at no risk.

CHAPTER

1

Range and Habitat

The Mute Swan has the most southerly breeding range of the Eurasian swans and, unlike the Bewick's and Whooper, many of the birds live in areas which are mild enough in winter for them not to have to migrate. Over the whole of its range, the bird has been so interfered with by man that it is impossible to say with any certainty what its original range was. Currently, it has a very fragmented distribution, breeding through many areas of north-central Europe, in areas in and around the Caspian and Azov Seas, in other parts of central Asia and as far east as parts of China.

Even within Europe the distribution of the Mute Swan is very patchy and scattered, and again it is not possible to say what its original range was. This stems largely from the fact that the birds must have been exterminated in many areas, while in the Mediaeval period virtually all of the Mute Swans in Britain and in several other areas were semi-captive. As we shall discuss later (Chapter 2), the birds were so valuable that almost all of them were owned by some local dignitary or other. The same situation held over wide areas of Western Europe, so that, for several centuries, it would barely have been true to consider the Mute Swan a wild bird at all. Only in the last century or so has the bird become once again a more or less wild bird.

All this keeping and rearing of birds and moving them about, coupled with fairly widespread hunting and persecution in other areas, means that the swan's current range may have little bearing on its original, natural, range. It has been suggested that the species is not a natural inhabitant of Britain, but that it was introduced, either perhaps by the Romans or, according to some, by Richard I after his return from the Crusades. Similarly, it has been suggested that the Mute Swan was introduced into Ireland (Kennedy *et al.* 1954). There seems to be no actual evidence to support these suggestions. Ticehurst discusses the possibility at some length in his book (1957: pages 2-7), and argues convincingly that the birds were already well established over a wide area by the time that Richard I returned from the Crusades and hence this suggestion at least can be discounted. We concur with Ticehurst's view that in all probability the birds were here of their own accord and were not introduced. After all, there was plenty of suitable habitat for them. In particular, the huge marshes in East Anglia would have provided ideal habitat. Further, our winters are much milder than those of most areas of Europe at similar latitude and so, even if at one time Mute Swans had not bred in Britain, almost inevitably birds would have found their way to Britain during particularly icy spells as they do today (see below). If they had done this, surely some would have taken a liking to these extensive marshes and would have stayed there?

The suggestion that the Mute Swan occurred naturally in Britain becomes even more likely when one considers that there was no English Channel immediately after the last Ice Age and therefore there was no sea barrier to birds moving into Britain until later. So, when our rich and extensive wetland habitats were forming after the retreat of the ice-cap, the birds would not even have had this short span of sea to cross.

Mute Swans are not great long-distance flyers; most of their movements are limited to the same river valley

Migrations and Movements

Although most British Mute Swans do not need to migrate long distances to reach mild areas for the winter, this is not the case for all Mute Swans elsewhere. Those which breed in parts of Russia and parts of northern

China simply cannot remain on their breeding grounds in winter; the areas become totally frozen over and inhospitable. The Mute Swans which live in these areas have to move southwards for the winter. Their migrations are poorly known, but many Russian birds move down to the large areas of open water such as the Black and Caspian Seas. Swiss ornithologists report an increase in Mute Swans during the winter, some of which may be of Russian or Polish origin.

Other populations, such as those in Sweden and some of the Baltic States, do not necessarily move very large distances. Those that live inland have to move because their breeding territories become completely frozen over during the winter. Many of these merely move down to the Baltic and spend the winter on the sea, which does not freeze; some also move south and west along the coasts. In some countries, such as Poland, almost all the swans depart for the winter and do not return until late March or April, when the ice on their breeding grounds has started to break up.

Some of these modest migrations may be extended in an unusually hard winter. For example, quite a few ringed Swedish birds have been recovered in Denmark in hard winters, and many birds from Eastern Europe have turned up in the west in harsh weather. In the very severe winter of 1939/40, ringed swans from Poland, Denmark, Germany and Sweden were found in Holland (van IJzendoorn 1951), while in the winter of 1962/63 several Continental birds turned up in Britain (see below). A study of Mute Swans ringed in Latvia and Lithuania has produced 140 recoveries in other countries as follows: Poland 4, East Germany 41, West Germany 17, Sweden 24, Denmark 43, Netherlands 1, Belgium 2, Britain 1, France 4, Switzerland 2, and Italy 1 (Jogi *et al.* 1974). The large majority of these recoveries were made during the three months January to March, the coldest part of the year.

Some of the young birds which migrate may stay on the wintering grounds when the adults return to their territories in the spring, and not head north again until a year later. Possibly, some of these find the wintering areas sufficiently acceptable for them to stay and breed there.

Movements of Swans between Britain and the Continent

Movements of Mute Swans across the North Sea and the English Channel are fairly infrequent. Nevertheless, some of the birds that turn up in coastal areas of Britain are very much more wary than the normal British birds, and these are particularly noticeable in very cold winters. Almost certainly, some of these are immigrants from the Continent. An early record of immigration is given in Yarrell (1845), who describes the arrival in Britain of a number of 'Polish Swans' (the colour variety, page 8) in the very severe winter of 1838; several flocks were seen 'pursuing a southern course along the line of our north-east coast from Scotland to the mouth of the Thames'.

Irrefutable evidence that some Mute Swans arrive in Britain from the Continent comes from ringing, but the indications to date from such studies suggest that movements into and out of Britain occur on only a modest scale. Some 50,000 swans have been ringed in Britain and large numbers in several other European countries, yet only a handful are known to have made the sea crossing. A high proportion of these can be associated with very harsh winters. For example, during the severe winter of 1962/63, two Mute Swans, ringed in Holland and Sweden, were recovered in Britain. Five swans ringed in Britain during that winter were subsequently recovered on the Continent: one each in Sweden, Holland, France, East Germany and West Germany. Presumably the birds left these countries during the freeze-up, came to Britain, where they were caught and ringed, and later returned to whence they came. Two other Mute Swans, ringed in Britain in the summer of 1963, were recovered on the Continent and may well have been birds that were delaying their return for one reason or another (these went to Holland and West Germany). During this very hard winter, birds from Denmark and Holland were also recovered in France. Similarly, three foreign-ringed swans (one Swedish, two Dutch) were recovered in Britain during the very severe weather in 1982.

The cross-channel movements are fairly restricted in that virtually all the birds that have made the journey have been recovered in, or ringed in, the southeastern coastal counties from Norfolk to Hampshire. In all (including the birds mentioned above), there are some 30 or more Mute Swans that have moved between these counties and Sweden, Denmark, Holland and France, with a few going as far east as Germany. One individual which does not fit this pattern is a bird ringed in Lithuania and recovered in Dumfriesshire. This swan was ringed as a juvenile in 1955 and recovered in Scotland in January 1959; it may of course have come in its first year and stayed on.

Dispersal within Britain

Ringing shows that most British Mute Swans tend to breed in the general area where they were raised. Permanent movements of more than 50 km are not common, and only some 3 per cent of birds move more than 100 km. Even those movements which do occur tend to take place within the same river system, suggesting that the birds do not like to venture far from water.

In a few cases whole broods seem to take it into their heads to move. The most striking case of this concerned a brood of eight cygnets which were ringed in Staffordshire. Of these, five were recovered in Glasgow and a sixth elsewhere in Scotland, strongly suggesting that the birds moved northwards as a family party, although why they should have made this unusual journey remains a mystery.

Seasonal Movements within Britain

Within Britain there are other seasonal movements in certain areas. Some of these are clearly related to changes in food supply (page 108) or to severe weather (page 93), and others to the search for territories (page 88). One which came to light only as a result of C.J. Spray's ringing of birds in the Hebrides is a small movement down the west coast of Scotland into Ireland during the winter. Although it looks as if this north-south movement may be fairly regular, there have been very few records of English-ringed swans moving westwards to Ireland.

In Scotland, as in Sweden, many birds come down to the coast for the winter (Church 1956). One of the main periods of the year when movements occur is just prior to, and just after, the moult, when non-breeding birds and failed breeders move to, and then return from, waters where they can be safe while flightless. Usually, this involves them in movements from small rivers to larger areas of water such as lakes, reservoirs and estuaries.

A critical requirement of these larger areas is that they must be ones where the birds can reach food easily without flying. Abbotsbury is a good example of such a place. There, there may be about 500 swans at the start of the breeding season, but up to 700-800 during the moult. After the moult, many of these visitors depart, but this emigration is soon followed by a further immigration and numbers build up to 1,000-1,200 by the end of the year (numbers reached as high as 1,500 in the early 1930s), after which they start to fall again. The winter influx includes many pairs with their broods (Perrins and Ogilvie 1981). We know that these birds come from a wide area of Dorset, Devon, Somerset and Wiltshire, but these areas are not thickly populated with swans and it is rather a puzzle as to where so many (600-700) swans come from.

Habitat

Mute Swans occupy a wide range of lowland wetlands. Their preferred natural habitat is probably mainly slow-flowing rivers and shallow, fresh-water marshes. The main requirements of the birds are a plentiful supply of aquatic vegetation within reach of their long necks when they 'up-end'. There is also some value in there being vegetation nearer the surface for the short-necked cygnets, but in many circumstances the adults will pull up vegetation for their young to feed on so that this may not be a serious problem.

In some areas, swans also nest in coastal sites, building nests of sea-weed on rocky promontories. Such sites are not uncommon in Sweden and a few are found in Scotland. They also occur in Denmark, but there this type of site became common only after the birds' numbers had built up at inland sites, suggesting perhaps that it is a less preferred habitat (Bruun 1960).

There is some puzzle about the Mute Swan's winter habitat. In late winter most aquatic vegetation dies down; nowadays in many areas the birds come out into fields to graze on grass or, if they live in towns, they may be dependent to a considerable extent on bread supplied to them by man. In primaeval Britain these foods would not have been available to them, so that exactly how they eked out a living in the lean months of the year is not clear. There will have been some suitable habitats for them such as saltmarshes where they may have been able to graze, but these would have been a long way from the inland waters where some of them would have bred and so would have involved them in journeys of far greater length than most inland birds seem to undertake today.

Another natural habitat which is used to some extent is shallow coastal waters, especially where the water is slightly brackish. In such places the birds can sometimes find plentiful supplies of eel-grass,

Zostera, and the tasselweeds, *Ruppia*. The swans that live on the Fleet in Dorset are highly dependent on these foods, as are those that breed in the Hebrides. In Denmark and Sweden, where the birds live in these habitats, these and other brackish-water plants may form an important part of the swan's diet (page 110). Before man changed the habitats, Mute Swans might have had to go to the coast in late winter to feed on these plants. Interestingly, the populations of Mute Swans in Denmark and Sweden have become abundant in these brackish habitats only in the very recent past; it is possible that earlier natural populations were exterminated (page 42).

Another important British habitat for the Mute Swan is a man-made one — gravel-pits. Although the greater part of most pits is usually too deep for there to be a rich growth of vegetation, the edges of these pits are often highly suitable. In addition, those with small islands in them provide highly desirable nesting habitats. The great increase in gravel-pits in many parts of the country has provided swans with a considerable amount of extra habitat.

Suitable nesting sites are an important part of any swan's territory and yet, in many areas, it is becoming particularly difficult for them to find such sites. The birds need a safe place where they can easily climb out of the water and build a nest. In the old marshes, this was not difficult. The birds could even flatten a small area of reedbed and build a more or less floating nest of reeds. On modern rivers this is much more difficult: reedbeds are scarce and banks tend to be steep, either dredged that way by waterways works or cut by the wake of passing boats. In many areas, more and more banks are being concreted to prevent further erosion. Once up on the bank, the swans find few places which are sufficiently secluded for their breeding requirements; there is a steady passage of people along the banks and few or no places where they can build a nest. Ideally — and wisely — they seem to prefer to nest on an island, since they can thus get a good measure of protection from interference and from attacks from foxes.

The habitat of the Mute Swan in many areas has changed markedly from what it was originally and, in most cases at least, not for the better from the swan's point of view. The degradation of habitat may, in the long term, be a serious factor limiting the chances that the Mute Swan will be able to maintain itself in certain areas. We shall return to this problem in later chapters (3 and 8).

CHAPTER
2
History and Customs

Introduction

The fact that the Mute Swan is a Royal Bird makes it unique. We have suggested that the Mute Swan was a natural endemic of the British Isles. Beyond that, there is little knowledge about the bird's ancient history in Britain.

We can only guess the course of events in the early stages. The swan must have lived successfully in the face of its natural enemies. The appearance of man, however, will have made a great difference to the situation. Presumably, the swans were originally just shot with arrows or trapped and eaten, as were other wild animals. Then, people realised that it was possible, with a little bit of planning, to round them up when they were flightless. Still later, perhaps, came the realisation that some could be kept, and subsequently eaten.

The keeping of swans, however, involved their owners in providing them with food. It would be easier still if they could be kept in such a way that they did not need feeding, provided that their owners could catch them whenever they wanted to. This problem was solved by pinioning them. Pinioning involves the amputation of the outer section of one wing so that the bird, lacking the main wing feathers, is flightless (this is a permanent effect; cutting the actual flight feathers also renders the bird flightless, but only until the next moult, when the bird grows new feathers and so can fly again). By using this technique, the owners of the swans could let them go in the rivers and leave them to fend for themselves, yet still recapture them at a later date.

There is not much point in owners letting the birds go unless there is

Plate 2. Swan uppers from the early 1900s

Plate 3. Today's swan uppers: from left to right — Bill Colley (The Vintners), John Turk (for the Queen) and Harold Cobb (The Dyers)

a high probability that they themselves will be able to recapture them later. Hence a complex system of ownership rules and a complex marking system grew up as a consequence of the pinioning and releasing. In this chapter we describe some of the traditions associated with swan ownership.

To the admirer of swans the habit of pinioning them may seem cruel and indefensible. Nevertheless, it is probably true to say that the Mute Swan would have been exterminated in Britain had it just been hunted and eaten like any other wild bird; it was so conspicuous and so easily caught. Banko (1962), quoting Dementiev and Gladkov, describes how, on the Caspian and Azov Seas, moulting swans are pursued until they are so exhausted that they can be clubbed to death. The fact that the Mute Swan could be managed in a semi-domesticated manner is almost certainly the reason why it has survived (page 38).

For several centuries, virtually all the swans in Britain were owned by someone; there would have been almost no wild, unpinioned swans. The fine sight of a Mute Swan in full flight, the wind singing through its wings, must have been a very rare spectacle in England for many centuries. That this is not just imagination is borne out by a statement in Yarrell (1845), writing of Abbotsbury: '... and as the cygnets are not caught to be marked and pinioned, the interesting sight of several of these fine large birds on the wing together is often witnessed.'

Early Ownership

The early history of Mute Swan ownership is lost in the mists of time; no written records remain. The customs associated with such ownership were obviously well established by the time of the earliest records which have survived. The history of the Mute Swan in captivity and the customs relating to keeping it have been well documented by N.F. Ticehurst (1957) in his book *The Mute Swan in England*. Much of this chapter is based largely on Ticehurst's findings.

At one time, the Crown claimed possession of all the swans in England. There is no record of when this was first decreed. As time passed, the Crown gave rights to the swans in certain areas to the local noblemen. The earliest statement about ownership which Ticehurst could produce was that of the year 966, when King Edgar gave the Abbots of Croyland rights over stray swans in their area. The significance of this statement lies in the implication that, if there were stray swans, there must have been others that were not stray, in other words birds that were owned by somebody. That they could be distinguished strongly suggests that they were marked in some way.

Giraldus Cambrensis, in an undated manuscript of the late twelfth century, possibly as early as 1186, describes the swan as a Royal Bird. In addition, the text refers to a number of swans living together on a water and belonging to the Bishop of Lincoln. By this date, however, swan-keeping had obviously been going on for some time, and in one sense the only peculiar thing about this record is that it has survived; there must have been many documents about swans by this date. Hence, as long ago as 966 people owned swans and presumably, as was always the case, the Crown had the say in who could and who could not own them.

Equally, long before 1186, large tracts of land were in the ownership of the local lord, and it is quite probable that those who owned areas with extensive waters acquired the rights of ownership of the local swans when they acquired the rights to the land. For example, the swans at Abbotsbury in Dorset have been the property of the Ilchester family for a very long time; the Ilchesters also own the stretch of water behind the Chesil bank, known as the Fleet, on which the swans live. The origins of the estate date back to 1023, when King Canute gave an area around Portesham to a man called Orc. This gift is presumed to have included the lands of Abbotsbury (adjacent to Portesham), since Orc founded the monastery there. At what point in time the swans came under the ownership of the monastery is unknown. The earliest known reference to the swans there is in 1393, when the Court Rolls of the Manor of Abbotsbury record that:

'William Squilor, keeper of the swans, stirred up the water under the bridge "de la Flete" with "les hacches" so that the water overflowed "le Flete" and is so high that it washed against the nests of the swans of the Lord and moved and destroyed the eggs of the Swans.'

The lord in this case was the Lord Abbot of Abbotsbury Monastery, but the fact that, by 1393, there was a 'keeper of the swans' and that there was a system of sluices to control the water level around the nests suggests that the birds had been tended for some considerable time prior to this date. Did Canute's gift in 1023 include the swans? All we can say for certain is that the swans have nested there in a man-controlled environment for virtually 600 years and possibly very much longer.

Swan Ownership

As the years went by, ownership rights were given by the Crown to many local Lords of the Manor or other dignitaries, although it was always a prerequisite of swan ownership that the person owned a sizeable area of land. At the height of swan-keeping there must have been very large numbers of swan owners. According to Ticehurst (1957), in 1553 there were upwards of 800 registered owners in one small section of the Fens. In 1871, at least ten people or bodies still laid claim to swans on the River Yare in Norfolk between Thorpe and Reedham (Stevenson 1890).

Enforcing the Law

The laws were enforced, often with severe penalties. The first known court case for stealing dates back to 1314, when four people were accused of (among other things) stealing two brood swans and five other swans (valued at £10) from the Bishop of Bath and Wells.

Ownership rights were also jealously guarded. The original Case Law concerning ownership of swans is often said to date back to 1592, when a case 'The Game of Swans' was brought against some people who claimed ownership of unmarked swans on the Fleet at Abbotsbury. The

Court established that the birds belonged to the Crown since they were on open waters and were not marked with any mark of ownership. As Ticehurst points out, however, the only real thing of interest about this case is that it is the earliest documented evidence that has survived to this day; by 1592 the rules must have been established for a very long time.

The earliest known set of rules is laid out in 'The Act for Swans', published in 1482. The next, the Witham Ordinance (relating solely to that river system), was published in 1524. This is important because later sets of rules bear marked similarities to this one and are plainly derived from it or, more probably, from a similar predecessor. In other subsequent sets of rules, the order of the rules varies and odd ones are included or omitted, but the substance remains largely the same. At the end of this chapter, we give an example of one of these sets of rules. This was published in 1563 and a copy exists in the Bodleian Library at Oxford. According to Ticehurst, there was an earlier version published some time during the reign of Edward VII (1547-53); there are very few changes between the two, the main one being that Rutland has been added to the version shown here. As mentioned above, some sets include other rules. The Witham Ordinance includes the following two rules of note which disappeared from later laws; in particular, it seems a pity that the second one disappeared!

'It is ordained, and by our laws made, that there shall be no fisher, or other man that have any ground butting on any water, or stream, where the swans may breed, or of custom have bred, shall mow, shear, or cut any thickets, reed or grass within 40 feet of the swan's nest, or within 40 feet of the stream, on pain of every such default, to forfeit unto the King, or his Deputy 40s.'

'It is ordained, and by our laws made, that there shall no hemp or flax be steeped in any running water, nor within 40 feet of the water, nor any other filthy thing be thrown in the running waters, whereby the waters may be corrupt, nor no man to encroach on the running water, whereby the waters may be hurt, by any kind of means, in pain for every such default, to forfeit unto the King or his Deputy 40s.'

The most complete gathering of these laws was published in 1632 and is given at the end of this chapter. These were not, strictly, laws but rather a set of guidelines produced by the Royal Swan Master. Presumably, however, they were much referred to at swan-upping and at swan meetings. It is interesting to speculate that these were probably published at least 600 years, and perhaps much longer, after the laws started to evolve!

Apart from having the right to all swans in England, except those which had been given away, the Crown also had control of who might be allowed to possess a swan-mark. In order to ensure that the laws were adhered to and the rather complex system administered, the Crown appointed an official, who was, and still is, known as Master of the Queen's (or King's) Game of Swans or the Royal Swan Master. The first known appointee was Thomas Gerveys, who exercised his duties on the Thames between London and Oxford in 1355. By the sixteenth century, it was usual practice for the Crown to bestow, as an honour, the title of Swan Master upon some favoured official. At that time it was a profitable post, since swan-keeping was big business.

The Swan Master had to organise the national management of the birds. The busiest time of year was the period in July when all the swans had to be 'upped'. Plainly, no one man could do this throughout the county on his own, so the Swan Master appointed deputies who were responsible for the different regions of the country; even so, they must have been much travelled people during swan-upping. Some districts were rented out to friends or colleagues. Nevertheless, the Swan Master had ultimate authority throughout the country except in the county of Lancaster, where, for some reason, the Duchy of Lancaster's Swan Marker had equal status.

The swan uppers in action. The whole swan family is caught and each bird is given an identification nick on its bill (the Queen's birds have no such mark)

The Swan Master's income came mainly from the charges which he could make to owners during swan-upping. Each year, all the new cygnets had to be caught and marked in order that their ownership could be established. This activity had to be supervised by the Swan Master or one of his deputies, so that no birds could be claimed unlawfully. A number of fixed charges were levied. First, the owner had to have his mark registered on the official swan roll; there was a charge of six shillings and eightpence for this, payable each time a swan-mark changed hands. In addition, there was a licensing charge of fourpence per year to keep any mark on the roll and a 'poll' charge of one penny for each adult and twopence for each cygnet caught.

Swan-marks

The swans could be claimed by an owner only provided that they were marked with his registered swan-mark. Any unmarked swan was the property of the Crown. The variety and complexity of these marks was impressive; we do not show the old marks here, but they are shown in Ticehurst's (1957) book. The first actual record of a swan-mark that Ticehurst could find relates to one in 1230, although marks must have existed long before that otherwise owners could not have separated their birds on common waters.

Many of these marks were very elaborate. Although most of them were made on the bill, marks on the wing and foot were also sometimes used, the latter especially if small cygnets were marked.

During the reign of Elizabeth I there were about 900 registered swan-marks. These were recorded on some 70 different swan rolls for different areas of the country. The only marks in use today are very inconspicuous: the Vintners and Dyers make a small nick in the fleshy side of the bill (one for Dyers, two for Vintners) and the Abbotsbury cygnets are marked by a tiny nick in the web.

In order to put the necessary marks on the new generation of swans each year, the broods had to be rounded up at swan-upping.

Division of the Broods

The ownership of swans was not strictly by area, but more by genealogy. The swans carrying an owner's mark belonged — as did their cygnets — to that owner whether they were on his or his neighbour's land, and similarly his neighbour's swans nesting on his land still belonged to his neighbour. Any swans (other than the cygnets of marked parents) caught at swan-upping but not bearing a proper mark could not be claimed if they were on open waters such as rivers; they belonged to the Crown. In practice, since the monarch obviously did not want the odd swan here and there, these birds were usually acquired by a local owner on payment of some agreed sum to the Crown.

The main aim of swan-upping was, of course, to claim the new year's young, and there were clearly laid-down rules about how the broods should be divided. In order to see fair play, all interested parties — the local owners (or their representatives) plus the Master of the King's Game of Swans or his deputy — had to be present during the upping. The Swan Master's representative was also responsible for organising the upping programme in each area, informing the interested parties, finding the necessary boats and any other administration. He was further responsible for recording each bird caught and adjudicating over the marking.

The disposition of the cygnets was fairly straightforward, although it seems to have varied a little from time to time and from place to place. If the parents of the cygnets both belonged to the same person and nested on his land, then he claimed all of them. If they nested on someone else's property, then one of the cygnets (the ground bird) went to the owner of that property as a repayment for the 'spoyle of his grasse'. Such a person might, by reason of owning insufficient land, not be entitled to own swans. When this was the case, then he was paid the value of the cygnet by someone who was entitled and who added the cygnet to his own stock.

When the two parents were the property of two different owners, the brood (after, if necessary, payment of a ground bird) was divided

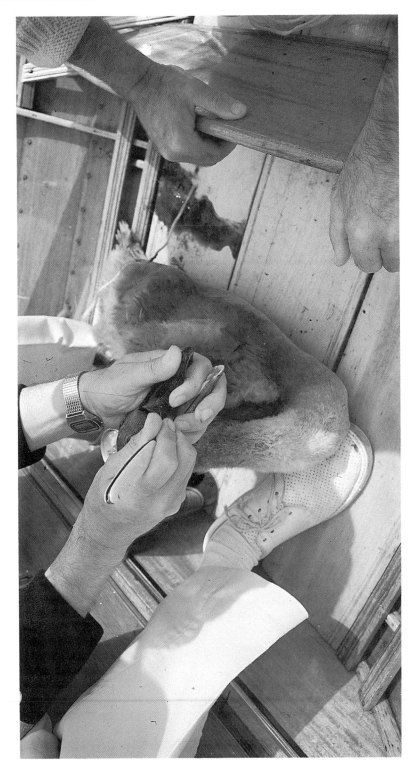

Plate 4. *Marking the cygnets. Today, the bill-marks are simple nicks in the bill, unlike the elaborate marks of the past*

G. R.

SWANS

£5 REWARD

The above Reward will be paid to any Person giving such information as shall lead to the conviction of the Person or Persons who shall

SHOOT AT, INJURE or DESTROY

ANY OF THE SWANS ON THE THAMES, OR

STEAL or DESTROY THEIR EGGS

Information should be furnished to any of the following:

Mr. F. T. TURK, His Majesty's Swan Keeper, "Rivergate," Cookham-on-Thames;
Mr. R. H. TURK, Vintners' Swan Marker, 289, King's Road, Kinsgton-on-Thames: or
THE DYERS' SWAN MARKER, Dyers' Hall, Dowgate Hill, London, E.C. 4;
AN INSPECTOR OF POLICE.

A man was convicted at Beaconsfield, May 27th, 1895, and sentenced to six weeks' hard labour for killing a Swan, and seven days' hard labour for stealing Swans' Eggs, and in October, 1908, another conviction took place, and a heavy fine inflicted, for shooting at and wounding Swans.

Harrison & Sons, Ltd., Printers in Ordinary to His Majesty, 44-47, St. Martin's Lane, London, W.C. 2. 11668r

Plate 5. Signs like these were common along the rivers of Britain some years ago. Similar signs can still be found at the locks on the River Thames

between them. One of the main variations concerned what happened to the 'odd' cygnet when the brood was not divisible by two. The odd one often went to the owner of the cob; sometimes two owners took it in turns to claim the odd one; and sometimes it was valued and whoever took it paid the owner of the other parent half its agreed value (this was often referred to as a half bird or a parting bird).

All the young swans were pinioned by removing the outer section of one wing. They were then marked with the owner's registered swan-mark. Some of the birds were released to maintain or increase the stock, while others were taken for fattening for the table. Those that were released had a bunch of feathers plucked from the tops of their heads in order to ensure that they were not needlessly caught again that year.

Cygnets which were taken off for fattening were kept in special swan-houses or swan-pits. Each region had its own swan-pit, a fenced-off area where the birds were fattened. The largest known swan-pit was in Norwich and belonged to St Helen's Hospital. It measured 74 ft by 32 ft (23 m × 10 m) and was at least 2 ft (0.6 m) deep. In this, St Helen's not only kept their own swans, but also bought in additional birds from local owners who had no pits of their own. This pit was used at least until 1880 and as many as 80-100 cygnets were kept there in a season. There were many such pits around the country; both King's College and Trinity College, Cambridge, are known to have had their own swan-pits.

Penalties

The Swan Master was also responsible for punishing those breaking the laws. There was a series of fines which could be imposed on the owners. If an owner turned up to upping without his swan-hook (an implement rather like a shepherd's crook, used for catching the birds), he was fined eightpence; if he left before completion of the catching, he was fined one shilling. Such misdemeanours, and any other disputes over swans, were dealt with at special swanning courts or Swan Motes. If any of the fines were not paid, the Swan Master was at liberty to take and sell as many of the owner's swans as was necessary to cover the fines.

Penalties for illegal owning of swans were much more severe; indeed, it was even a punishable offence to be found carrying a swan-hook without authority. Anyone who stole a swan's egg could be imprisoned for a year and a day and fined at the will of the King (half the fine going to the King, the other half to the owner of the land where the eggs were taken, so encouraging reporting of the deed).

Even in quite recent times, fines have been severe. A man was convicted in 1895 at Beaconsfield of killing a swan; he was sentenced to six weeks' hard labour and a further seven days for stealing the eggs (Plate 5).

Some of the penalties seem very harsh by today's standards, especially when one considers the average wages that were earned at that time. Against this, however, must be set the value of the birds, the fact that they were often on open waters and not easily guarded, and the fact that penalties for many other offences were even higher. With regard to the value of the birds, we have already cited the case where a breeding pair and five other swans were valued at £10 in 1315. Ticehurst (1957) quotes two more modest sums: in 1505, two cygnets were valued at four shillings and eightpence the two (roughly eight for £1) and a single cygnet sold for two shillings (10p).

Catching a swan can be made easier by using a long swan-hook

The Swan Laws

The following texts are examples of the old laws mentioned in this chapter. Both are identical to their original, except that we have 'translated' various words whose meanings might not have been clear.

The first is a copy of the early Swan Laws. The earliest set of these is the so-called Witham Ordinance (which deals only with that river system). Several versions are known, all of which bear a strong resemblance to each other and are clearly based on the Witham Ordinance (or, more probably, on earlier documents which are no longer in existence). This text is taken from a copy in the Bodleian Library, Oxford. It was printed in the sixth year of Queen Elizabeth (i.e. 1563/64). There is a predecessor to this document, issued during the reign of Edward VII (1547-53); the two are more or less identical except that Rutland has been added to the list of counties. It is virtually the same as the Witham Ordinance except that two rules have been dropped.

This is the ordinance for the conservation and keeping of the queens majesties swannes and sygnettes, and of the Lords Spiritual and Temporal and of her commons with the counties of Lincolne, Northampton, Rutland, Huntingdon and Cambridge, and the liberties and franchises of the game: and for the conservation of fishe and fowle with the assisting [?] all manner of nets within the said counties and liberties of the same.

First it is ordained and stated that any person having any Swannes, shall begin yearly to mark or cause to be marked the same upon the

Sunday next after Trinity Sunday, no person afore, but after as the company may, so that the Master of the Queens Game of Swannes, or his deputies be there present, and if any person or persons take upon him or them in marking to the contrary, to forfeit to the Queene 40s.

It is ordained that no person or persons being Swanheards nor other, shall go on marking without the master of the Queens game of Swannes or his deputy be present with six or four of the company of Swanheards upon pain to forfeit to the Queens grace 40s.

It is ordained that no person shall take up no cygnet nor cygnets unmarked, nor make no sale of them but with the Queens Swanheard or his deputy with four other swanheards next adjoining be present or have knowledge of the same to forfeit to the Queens grace 40s.

It is ordained that the Swanherd of the Duchy of Lancaster within the said counties, nor within the liberties and franchises of the same, nor no other person for him nor by him, shall make no sale nor take up no Swannes nor mark them within the said Duchy without the Queens Swanherd or his deputy be present upon pain to forfeit to the Queens grace 40s. And in likewise it is ordained that the Queens Swanherd of the aforesaid counties nor his deputy shall not enter into the said Duchy to take up any Swans or Cygnets, nor to mark them without the Swanherd of the Duchy be present, upon pain to forfeit to the Queens grace 40s. It is ordained that if any cygnets be found without the said duchy double-marked or put out of the right mark, that they shall be seized for the Queen and to be delivered to the Master of the Queens game of Swannes or his Deputy and so to remain to it be proved by four or six sufficient swanherds to whom the same swans or cygnets belong or appertain, so that the knowledge of the same be had by the said Swanherds after the said delivery afore the sessions of Swannes than next to be kept within the countie whereas it shall hap the said swans or cygnets to be seized and delivered in form aforesaid. And if so be the property of the same Swannes and cygnets cannot be known by the said sessions, that then the Queen be assured of the value of the same swans and cygnets.

It is ordained that if any person or persons wilfully put any swans from their nest wheresoever they breed or else take up and destroy or bear away any eggs or egg of the said swans to forfeit for every default presented in the sessions of swans to the Queens grace 13s 4d.

It is ordained that no man shall make sale of no white swans, nor make delivery of them without the Master of the Game or his deputy be present, with four or six swanheards next adjoining under pain of 40s whereof shall be to the finder 6s.8d and the residue to the Queen.

It is ordained that no person or persons hunt in fence time or in any haunt of swans with dogs from the feast of Easter to the Sunday after Trinity Sunday on pain of every time so doing 6s 8d.

It is ordained that if any person set any snares or any manner of engines to take bittorns or swannes between the feast of Easter and Lammas he or they to forfeit for every time so setting any such engines 6s 8d.

It is ordained that no person nor persons shall lay no net nor nets within the common streams, waters nor marshes upon the day time, from the feast of the Inuention of the holy cross, unto the feast of Lammas, upon pain as often as they be found in fault and presented in the sessions of swannes before the Queens Justices, 20s to forfeit to the Queens grace.

It is ordained that any swanherd intending to keep any swans or cygnets, that they shall keep them within a pen or pit within 20 feet of the common stream or else within 20 feet of the Queens highway, so that the Queens subjects passing by may have the sight of the said swans upon pain of 40s.

It is ordained that there shall be no forfeit of white swans nor grey swans nor cygnets but only to the Queens grace, as well within the franchises and liberties as without: and as often as any person seize and deliver the said swannes to any other person, but only to the master of the game or to the Queens use, he to forfeit to the Queens grace 6s.8d.

It is ordained, that no manner of person or persons shall lay nor set trammels, nor nets called drages, nor drag with no net from the 16th day next before the feast of St Mark the Evangelist until the 16th day next ensuing the same feast. That is to wit, within the common streams, waters, fens and marshes in the County of Lincoln, Southampton, Rutland, Huntingdon, and Cambridge nor within the Isle of Ely, upon pain of 40s.

It is ordained that no man shall take no gray swans nor white swans flying, but that he shall within four days next after the said taking, deliver them to the Master of the Queens Swans or to his deputies to the Queens use, and the taker to have for his taking 8d.

It is ordained that no manner of person of what estate, degree, or condition he be, having any game of swans of his own shall be no swanheard nor keeper of none other mens swans, upon pain of 40s.

It is ordained, that no swanheard nor fisher, nor fowler, shall not vexe nor trouble another swanheard nor fisher nor fowler by way of action or otherwise, but only alone the Queens Justices of her sessions of swans, upon pain of forfeiting to the Queens grace 13s.4d.

God Save the Queen

Imprinted in London in Powles Churchyard by Richard Jugge and John Cawood, Printers to the Queens Majesty.

The following text is from a small document which is a set of the rules produced by the Royal Swan Master in 1632. Strictly speaking, it is not law, but it seems to have become the working guidelines for swan-upping and was much referred to. The lead-in to this paper is a letter from John D'Oyly, himself an ex-Thames Swan Master. D'Oyly not only points out that a countrywide set of rules was badly needed since different areas had different rules, but he also makes clear that the different areas could be given freedom to modify certain parts of the rules, but not others.

THE ORDERS LAWS AND ANCIENT CUSTOMS OF SWANS

Caused to be printed by John Witherings Esquire, Master and Governour of the Royall Game of Swans and Signets throughout England.

London Printed by August Mathewes 1632.

[The following is the letter from John D'Oyly]

To the Worshipful John Witherings Esquire, chief Master and Governour of the Royal Game of Swans and Cygnets, throughout the Kingdom of England.

Sir, Your deputie Master Loggins, hearing that I had some ancient notes of the Customes and Orders concerning swans, desired me that you might have a sight of them which I have sent you together with certain Presidents or forms of Commissions for keeping Swanheard Courts and Copies of ancient Patents which I received of a very honest gentle-man Master Edward Clerke (Lord Buckhurst's Deputy Swan-Master for the River Thames) of Lincolnes Inn Esquire, father to Sir Edward Clerke one of the Masters of the Chancery. These he delivered mee about 18 years ago at which time Sir Lawrence Tanfield late Lord Chief Baron, and my self had a deputation from Sir William Andrewes, of that walke which Master Loggins now hath from you. Master Clerke was before mee, but as I remember he told me he had his deputation from my Lord of Buckhurst (Master of Swans at the end of 16th Century) and not from Sir James Merrin. Howsoever, the titles are truly by mee transcribed, as I received them written with his own hand. There are Orders also Printed, and yet somewhat differing from these, which Orders were made at one particular Court long ago. And at a Court holden at Burford in the county of Oxon about 15 years ago by the said Sir Lawrence Tanfield and others, some new Orders were made; which Sir Lawrence Tanfield said were Warrantable by the Commission, and lawfull to be made, where and when they were fit and necessary for the preservation of Swans. Yet so that those particular Orders may bee altered upon occasion: but the ancient Customes contained under the Orders may not. There has beene so little care taken for preserving and publishing these ancient customs that they are not of all Gamesters known. And your Deputies commonly send their servants among us, who as they are more or lesse covetous, so do they impose more or lesse upon us: and when wee that are the ancient gamsters oppose them, wee have some contention. You shall therefore (Sir) doe well if comparing these with your other notes you finde them to serve generally for England as well as for our river of Thames: that you give to all your Deputies, and to all Commissioners copies, that so all gamsters may know the certaine Customes which are to be kept: and so I bid you heartily Farewell.

Your Loving friend

John D'Oyly

From Alborne in Wiltshire

this 26th of January 1631

These Orders to Master Doyly his direction, I have examined and compared with some other Orders which are now in print; and have been observed and used in some parts of this Kingdome: but I finde anciently used these Laws Customs and Orders in most parts of this Kingdome, and not much differing from those Orders now Printed, in matter of substance, but onely in forme. As also I finde a Commission used for the preservation of the Royal Game of Swanns and Signets directed to Noble-men, Knights, and Gentle-men, for the enquiry of abuses committed contrary to these Laudable Orders and Customes, and the offences to punish according to their several qualities, and have caused these Orders to bee printed that thereby better knowledge may be taken of them by every deputy Master of the Game.

John Witherings

THE LAWS ORDERS AND CUSTOMES FOR SWANS, taken forth of a book which the Lord of Buckhurst delivered to Edward Clerke of Lincolnes Inn Esquire, to peruse An.Eliz.26. (1632) On the backside of which book: it was thus intituled

Taken out on an Ancient book remaining with Master Hambden, sometimes Master of the Swannes [probably either Sir John Hampden (knighted 1513) or Edward Hampden (died 1570); both were Thames swan owners].

First, if any person doth possesse any Game of Swannes, that may not dispend five Marks a yeere of Freehold (except the son of the King) the Swannes of every such person are forfeit to the King: 22.Edward 48.

2. If any person possesse any Game of Swannes, and hath not payd his fine [fee] for the same: his Game of Swans is to be seazed for the King, till his fine be payd. Which fine is Sixe shillings and eightpence, and no man is to pay it more than once during his life.

3. But if any person having no Marke allowed him, has one or more Swannes given him, or have any Land-bird figne marked [a temporary mark]: he may keep them in the common River till the next Upping time (without fine) paying the Commons and the other charges for the Upping.

4. If any person having Swannes, either within Franchises or without be attainted, his Swannes are forfeit to the King onely, and not to any other person whatsoever.

5. Also all Swannes that are clear of Bill, without mark or figne mark, are the Kings onely, whether they be pinioned or flying Swannes.

6. Also all stray Swannes which no man can challenge by his mark, those are the Kings onely. And they are to be seazed for the King, and marked on the legge, but are not to be caryed away the first yeare.

7. In all the Common streams and private waters when Cignets are taken up, the owner of the Cob must choose the first Cignet, and the Pen the next, and so in order. But if there be three, then the owner of the Grasse where they breed, must have the third, for the spoil of his Grasse: and must pay to the King Twelve pence for the same Land-bird, saving in such places where of ancient custom they pay less, or more.

8. If an Heire [brood] be ledd by one Swanne onely, the half of those Cignets shall be seazed for the King, till proofe be made whose the Swanne was that is away; but are not to be caryed away that year.

9. The Master of the Game or his Deputy shall yearely come at the usuall days of marking Swannes in that streame (on pain of losing his Fees during his absence). And he shall keepe a Roll or standard book, containing all the usual markes of that streame. He shall also keep a Register booke of the numbers of every mans Swannes and the place where they are upped. And shall likewise bring the book of the last yeere. For which every Gamster is to give him yearly, Fourpence.

10. Also the Master of the Game, or his Deputy is to have a penny for upping every white Swanne and two pence for every Cignet, and shall have his dinner and supper, and hay or grass for his Horse discharged by the Gamsters every Upping day, except in such streames where by ancient custome other composition is used.

11. If any man desire the Master of the Game to enter any note in his book (other than the notes due to be written as aforesaid) or to take any note out of his book under his hand, he is to pay for the same 4 pence.

12. If any marked Swanne be unpinioned, and thereby doe or may fly, the Owner of that Swanne is to pay Foure-pence. And if any man take any flying Swanne or Cignet, he must bring the same to the Master of the Game or his Deputy and take for his pains 8 pence on pain of Fortie shillings.

13. It is ordained that no person shall lay any lepes [?loops = snares], set any Nettes or Dragge within the Common streames or Rivers upon the day time from the Feast of the Inuention of the Cross [May 3rd] unto the Feast of Lammas [August 1st], upon pain so often as they shall be found so offending to forfeite 20 shillings.

14. If any Swanne be found double-marked, embezeled, or by unskil-fulnesse put out of right mark, the Master of the Game is to choose five Gamsters (who are indifferent) to judge who has right to that Swanne. And hee to whom the Swanne shall bee adjudged, shall pay Foure-pence for registering the said embezeled or wrong mark. But if those five, or the greater number of them doe not adjudge the said Swanne to one of the Gamsters, then the Swanne is due to the King.

15. The usual days of Upping of Swannes are not to be altered with-out consent of the greater number of Gamsters of that streame, and that by Proclamation made in all market Townes near the said streame.

16. No person shall goe on marking without the Master of the game, or his Deputy bee present upon pain to forfeit Fourtie-shillings. But if by sicknesse or other occasion, he be absent at the usual Upping days, the company may goe on so that some sworn Gamster keepe the Register book, and receive all the dues, and deliver them to him at his coming.

17. If any person doe embezele, raze, or alter the mark of any Swanne, to the loss or hindering of any man's game, he shall suffer one yeares imprisonment, and be fined three pounds, six shillings and eightpence and for ever be disabled to be a Gamster.

Plate 6. Swan-upping. Members of the Queen's boat grab one of the adult birds

18. And to the end that at Upping-time no swan be embezeled, it is ordained that no man draw blood of any swanne, till the Master of the Game or his Deputy has viewed the said swanne, and declared whose the swanne is.

19. No swanne (other than clear-billed) [i.e. unmarked] is to be marked for the King on the beake, but onely on the legge. For two markes on the beake are unlawfull.

20. The Master of the Game may presently fell or carry away all swannes that are clear-billed, embezeled (as aforesaid) and all swannes forfeit for want of Freehold, or by attaint of the Owner.

21. And yet neither the Master of the Game, nor any other Gamster may take away any swanne which is in broode with any other mans, or which is coupled, and has a walk, without the others consent, for breaking the broode.

22. It is ordained that Commons, that is to say, dinner and supper is to be paid daily by every Banker or Commoner, whether he bee present or absent. But if he be absent, the Master of the Game is to lay it out for him (as likewise all other dues) till their next meeting or Upping. But the said Commons shall not exceed above Twelve-pence a man. And if the Company will spend more they are to pay the overplus, by the Poll.

23. To the end that diet may be had at reasonable rate, and likewise lodging; the place of taking both, is to be chosen by the greater number of the Commoners.

24. If any person be found carrying a Swan-hooke within forty lugg [one-eighth of a mile] of any streame, saving on the Upping days, and not accompanied with two swan-herdes, he shall forfeit Thirteene-shillings foure pence. But upping on the Upping days, every Gamster that caryeth not a Hooke (except such gentlemen as for pleasure goe to see their owne game) shall forfeit eight pence a day, the one half to bee for the Master of the Game, the other halfe for the Company.

25. No person shall take up any Swanne or Cignet, marked or unmarked, unlesse it be done in the presence of two other swan-herdes, and that by allowance of the Master of the Game, or his Deputy, for which allowance he is to pay Foure-pence upon pain to forfeit Fourtie shillings.

26. If any swan-herdes depart before he hath made even with the Master of the Game, for all dues, he is to forfeit Twelve-pence: For which, as for all dues, the Master of the Game or his Deputy may distrain the Game: and at the next Upping may pay himself by distraining and sale of the Game, rendering to the party the overplus.

27. If there bee any person or persons that hath Swannes, that do heirie [breed] upon any part of their Rivers, or severall waters; and afterwards come to the common water or River, they shall pay a Land-bird to the King, and be obedient to all Swan-lawes: for divers such persons do use collusion to defraud the King of his Right.

28. If any person shall take away the egge or egges of any swanne: Every such Offender shall be imprisoned a yeere and a day; and shall pay Thirteen shillings Fourepence for every Egg so taken away. Whereof halfe to the King and halfe to Owner of the swan. II of Henry 7.

29. If any person doe drive away any Swanne breeding or providing to breed, be it on his owne ground or any other mans: he shall be fined 13.s.4d. and shall suffer one yeares imprisonment. II of Henry 7.

30. If any Dogge shall drive any Swanne away from her nest, the Owner of such Dogge shall forfeit Thirteene shillings foure pence. But if any Dogge shall kill any old Swanne; the Owner of such Doggie shall forfeite to the King Fouretie shillings. Whether he be there or not.

31. If any person shall hunt any Ducks, or any other chase in the water with any Dogge or Dogges in fence time [? close season]; (that is from the feast of Easter till Lammas Eve) he shall pay for every offence, sixe shillings eight pence.

32. It is ordained that if any person doth set any Snares or any manner of Nets, Lime or Engines, to take Bittorns [? Herons] or Swans, from the Feast of Easter to the Sunday after Lammas day: Hee or they to forfeite to the Kings Majestie for every time so setting 6.s.8.d.

33. If there be any weirs upon the Rivers, not having grates before them, whereby the Swannes or Cignets may be defended from drowning: the Owner of such Weir shall forfeite to the King thirteene shillings foure pence.

34. All Fisher-men are to assist the Master of the Game or his Deputy, in the execution of their Office on the Upping days, with their boats at the upper end of their several waters, upon pain of tenne shillings for every default. For which service the Master of the Game shall cause the accustomed Fees to be paid to the said Fisher-men.

35. Lastly, if there be any other Misdemeanoure, or Offence committed, or done by any Owner of any Game, Swan-heard, or any other person whatsoever, contrary to any Lawe, ancient Custome, or usage heretofore used and allowed, and not before herein particularly mentioned or expressed, you shall present the same Offence, that reformation may be had, and the Offendors punished, according to the quantity and quality of the several Offences.

At every Swan-heards Court, all Offences committed by breach of these orders, are to be enquired of.

Note that the Swan-heard for the Duchy of Lancaster is to observe and see observed, all these orders in his circuit, and to receive the fees belonging to the King's Swan-heard.

Note that in all forfeitures to the King, a fourth part is due to him that gives information of the offence.

Note that none is to go as a Swan-upper, but those who are sworn, if Courts be often kept.

FINIS
GOD SAVE THE KING

CHAPTER
3
Swan Numbers

A pair of Mute Swans looking for a nest site

The Distant Past

Sadly, we know little about the numbers of swans that have been present in Britain over the centuries. In Chapter 2 we follow Ticehurst (1957) in suggesting that Mute Swans must have been endemic to, and well established in, Britain long before man arrived on the scene. It seems almost certain, however, that, after man arrived and started to hunt in the marshes, the swans would have undergone a dramatic decline in numbers. Ticehurst points out that many other large species were more or less exterminated as man became more numerous and as his hunting prowess and equipment increased. He suggested that only the domestication of the Mute Swan saved it from a similar fate.

Ticehurst goes on to suggest that, once man discovered that he could 'crop' the swans instead of merely hunt them, swans would have increased in numbers. With their being so valuable and there being so many owners, there must have been enormous numbers of swans alive in all the river systems during the period when they were in 'domestication', and certainly more than there ever were before or have been since.

In view of the swans' value, it is surprising that there are not more records of their numbers in the early documents. It seems a little odd that the Crown's Swan Keeper and his deputies should have been so concerned with keeping the rules of ownership and the records of ownership that they did not, at the same time, keep records of the numbers of birds possessed by each owner. There are a few much-quoted statements that indicate the numbers there might have been during the height of swan-keeping. Yarrell (1845) quotes two early authors. One, Paulus Jovius, said in 1543 that he had 'never seen a river so thickly covered with swans as the Thames'. The other was John Taylor, who, in 1625, made a longish journey along several rivers, during which he passed up the Avon to Salisbury; describing this stretch, he said that 'at the least 2,000 swans, like so many pilots, swam in the deepest places before us, and showed us the way'.

We would add only one word of caution: numbers such as those recorded would have needed impressive amounts of food to maintain them. For example, individual swans eat something of the order of 4 kg of water plant per day; alternatively, they may eat something in excess of 0.5 kg of grain. Hence a flock of 2,000 swans would require a very considerable amount of food. A flock as large as this would certainly have needed some sort of feeding by the owners during the winter. In mid-winter, they may well have been able to get some of their food from poorly drained water meadows where they were not too seriously in competition with other stock such as cattle. As soon as the water level dropped in spring, however, there would have been great conflict between the owners of cattle and horses and the swans. Once again nothing seems to have been recorded, but we merely wish to emphasise that there may be some danger in assuming that swans were quite as numerous as the few reports suggest.

Ticehurst located a few records of numbers which certainly seem to support the idea that Mute Swans were very common at this time. In 1553, 'a small corner of the Fenland' contained 35 broods of 183

Plate 7. Today, the only place in Britain where hundreds of Mute Swans can be seen together is Abbotsbury in Dorset

cygnets; the results of multiplying this up suggest that there might have been as many as 5,500 cygnets in a total swan population in the Fenland of about 24,000. This is rather larger than the whole British population of today! Although realising the dangers inherent in such computations, Ticehurst thought that this figure was probably an underestimate.

In 1696, there were 44 broods of 197 cygnets on the old Ouse between Willingham and Ely. In 1697, there were 25 broods with 108 cygnets on an eight-mile (13-km) section of the two Bedford rivers between Earith Bridge and Welches Dam. In 1587, there were 41 broods on the Lea between Tottenham and Stortford, indicating, according to Ticehurst, a population of about 700 swans on the Lea and its tributaries. If these scanty records are to be interpreted in this way, then the large numbers recorded by Paulus Jovius and John Taylor may well be true.

Similarly, the large numbers of swans, presumably all cygnets, eaten at banquets also indicate that the stocks must have been large. Many people ate them regularly at their Christmas feast. Henry III had at least 125 for Christmas in 1251, but the record for a feast seems to have been 400 at the installation of George Nevell as Archbishop of York in 1466.

It would also be of interest to know more about how the birds were farmed. How many of the young were removed for fattening and how many was it thought necessary to keep to maintain the stock? Ticehurst reports that in 1553 Sir William Cecil rounded up 90 cygnets between Croyland and Whittlesey (Norfolk). Of these he sold 39 and kept 51 to 'increase his game'. We have no idea whether or not this was the sort of proportion that was normally kept, but, if 50 per cent of the birds were taken and the other half left, then, with an average brood-size of about four, the produce of 200 pairs would have been needed to provide 400 cygnets for a feast.

Decline in Swan-keeping

Gradually, as living standards increased and, probably more importantly, as other, easier to keep, birds became available, the swan's value as a source of food diminished. In particular, the domestic goose — a descendant of the wild Greylag — became widespread. The Turkey seems to have been first introduced into Britain at some time between 1525 and 1532. These two birds, together with the domestic hen and to a lesser extent the guineafowl, were much easier to keep and were probably to a large extent responsible for the decline in popularity of the swan.

The swan had two major drawbacks as a domestic animal. First, the aggressive nature of the cobs made it impossible to keep them at high density and, second, they flourished really only if they had ready access to water. In addition, if they were released on open waters, the trouble involved in recapturing them, sorting out who owned them and, doubtless also, the loss rate from poaching and other hazards made birds such as the Turkey and the guineafowl much easier subjects for domestication.

Presumably, as the Mute Swan fell from favour as a table delicacy its numbers declined. No longer jealously guarded, it was still fair game for anyone who wanted an easy meal and, since the old laws were no longer so rigorously enforced, there was little risk in taking swans. Doubtless therefore, although records are scarce, the numbers fell greatly during the succeeding years. Ticehurst considered that, by the mid-eighteenth century, swan-keeping had more or less ceased in most parts of the country and that 'it was only being kept alive by a few of the largest land-owners'.

Swan ownership lasted a little longer than this in one or two places, particularly the Fens. There, the birds were farmed until at least the end of the century. The following is based on Stevenson (1890), who went on the swan-upping on the River Yare in 1871 and gathered information from the swanherds. At that time, many private owners were still claiming rights to swans although most, including Norwich Town Council, had given up having swanherds of their own. Norwich delegated the swanherd's duties to a man named Simpson, who also ran the St Helen's Hospital swan-pit where the swans were fattened. At least ten people or bodies laid claim to swans on the River Yare between Thorpe and Reedham, and ownership of the birds was still based on marks on the birds' beaks.

Swans were clearly quite abundant at that time, since something from 100 to 150 birds were taken for fattening each year and several broods were always left on the streams as they were surplus to requirements. Such a crop indicates a minimum of 30 pairs or so even if all the cygnets were taken, and, assuming that only about half of them were removed, then the breeding population must have been nearer 60 pairs. The value of an 'upped' cygnet was ten to twelve shillings and each owner paid Simpson a guinea for fattening it; the market value of a fattened cygnet was about two guineas.

Today, only the swans on the Thames and those at Abbotsbury are claimed and we discuss something about both these areas elsewhere (page 48 and page 78).

The Numbers of Mute Swans in Europe

We shall discuss the numbers of swans in Britain later in this chapter, but here we look briefly at the history of the Mute Swan in Europe during the last century or so.

We do not have good data on their status in the nineteenth century, but Britain was not the only country whose people discovered that swans could be easily caught while they were flightless, or that they could be pinioned and farmed. Certainly, people in other countries managed the swans in much the same way that they were managed in Britain. For example, van IJzendoorn (1951) claims that there were no wild Mute Swans in Holland for a long period of time and that at certain periods, such as the sixteenth century, the birds could be owned only by noblemen. Similarly, Mayaud (1962) describes the birds as being well established on several rivers in the vicinity of Paris in the late seventeenth century. At least some of these were owned, since there were annual round-ups when the cygnets were shared out.

Elsewhere, they were, being edible, much hunted. Such hunting is described by Dementiev and Gladkov (1951) for the Caspian area;

moulting birds were chased until exhausted and then clubbed down. The most graphic account of such a hunt that we know of is given by Lloyd (1854), describing a large round-up of Mute Swans in Sweden (Plate 8). These round-ups took place in bays along the Baltic coast where large numbers of swans congregated for the moult; some of the flocks contained 1,000 to 1,200 birds. The following is an extract from his account:

'in the olden time — in the palmy days of powder-puffs, etc. — several grand battues were annually got up, in the moulting season, for the capture of the mute swan ...' (swan skins at this time were, according to Lloyd, equal in value to those of the fox) '... the peasants are compelled by law to lend a hand on these occasions ... The day and place of rendezvous ... having been publicly notified ..., the men assemble at the appointed hour, usually about midnight ... The flotilla proceeds at break of day to the scene of action ... When the bay on which hostilities are to be carried on is reached, the boats separate; and each taking up its appointed station, a Cordon is formed completely across its entrance, and thus the swans are imprisoned as it were ... When however, the swans perceive the approach of the enemy ... they make every effort to escape from the toils. Such as can fly take wing and face for the open sea, in their way to which they are exposed to a murderous fire from the boats; whilst the others, usually the major portion of the flock, being unable, for want of sufficient feathers, to rise above the water, either take to the strand where they are captured living by the land party, or dash between the boats.'

Those that did escape between the boats were chased and captured, or shot when they became exhausted enough to allow the boats to get within range.

Lloyd reports that well-organised hunts, involving some 40 or more boats, sometimes took upwards of 600 swans (although the actual hunt on which he went did not, since it was too late in the season and most of the birds could fly). Lloyd noted that the birds did not breed in any numbers either in southern Sweden or in Denmark at that time, and questioned where all these swans came from. He concluded, largely on the evidence of the local fishermen who saw birds flying in before the moult, that most of them came from countries on the east coast of the Baltic or farther east. Conforming with the view that they were not locally bred, he noted that 'young birds are never seen in these hunts — the plumage of all being white or nearly so'. There were, however, clearly plenty of one-year-old birds, since Lloyd says that 'And what seems singular, the number of males and females is about equal — the bills of the males being yellow-red whilst those of the females are liver-brown.' The latter are, of course, the one-year-old birds, not the females.

Presumably, hunts of this sort went on in other areas, wherever swans were common enough to make it worthwhile to organise them. In areas where they were rarer, they would have been shot. It is hardly surprising, therefore, that the Mute Swan remained very scarce in many areas of Europe for much of the early part of this century. If there were areas where the birds started to build up in numbers, doubtless the hunger

Plate 8. A plate from Lloyd's (1854) book illustrating a scene at one of the annual round-ups of swans along the Baltic coast. Flightless birds were clubbed to death, while the flyers were shot

caused by the two World Wars resulted in many losses. In these conditions, any swan would have been a very tempting item, whatever the conservation laws might have been at the time.

Nowadays, Mute Swans are much commoner than they were at the beginning of the century; they have increased over large areas of Europe. The timing of the increases seems to have varied in different countries, and has usually been associated with a change in legislation giving more protection to the Mute Swan. For example, in Denmark there were only three or four pairs in 1925. After being given full protection in 1926, they increased steadily, reaching some 2,700-3,000 pairs by the mid-1960s; over a long period they were increasing at about 18 per cent per annum. The birds tended to increase in the lakes and rivers first, and then spread onto fiords and other coastal waters (Bruun 1960). Similarly, the Mute Swan was very rare in Sweden in the 1920s, but afterwards showed an 'explosive' increase up to the 1960s, this increase involving the birds spreading out into coastal areas and breeding in the brackish waters of the Baltic (Winge 1959, Terras-Wahlberg 1960, Berglund *et al.* 1963).

In areas of Eastern Europe, such as Poland, the increase seems to have been mostly post-war, many birds having presumably been taken for food during the war (Sokolowski 1960). In Estonia, the Mute Swan was exterminated around 1928 and did not breed for about another 30 years (Kumari 1970); it then started to breed again in 1959 (Ling 1961) and has increased since then. Jogi *et al.* (1974) put the breeding population of Estonia, Lithuania and Latvia at over 285 pairs. In some of these areas the population is still clearly increasing, though the Mute Swan seems to be getting near to the northerly limit of its range, because of the harshness of the winters.

Cramp and Simmons (1977) give the populations of various European countries as follows: Ireland 5,000-6,000 birds, France 200-300 pairs, Denmark 2,740 pairs, Norway up to 20 pairs, Sweden up to 2,500 pairs, Finland about 20 pairs, West Germany over 1,500 pairs, East Germany nearly 1,000 pairs, Poland 3,600 pairs, Switzerland nearly 250 pairs, Netherlands 2,500 pairs, and USSR 4,600 pairs (3,000 around the Caspian). Some of the censuses on which these figures are based were made over 20 years ago, and so these numbers may well not accurately portray the present position. Currently, the total population of Europe in winter is thought to be over 140,000 birds, and a further 10,000 may winter outside Europe in the Black Sea area.

The Numbers of Mute Swans in Britain

As we have mentioned, people have taken the Mute Swan for granted to such an extent that very few attempts have been made to count the birds. By far the best long-term figures for swan numbers are those for the Thames, and we discuss these in the next part of this chapter. During the last 30 years, there have been three main attempts to census the British population of Mute Swans. It is interesting to note that the 1955-56 census was made because of complaints that there were too many swans, while those in 1978 and 1983 were made after complaints that swans were becoming too scarce in many areas! Each of these counts took place in spring, so that only fully grown birds and not cygnets were counted.

The 1955 census covered most of England, Wales and Scotland, but some areas that were missed were counted in 1956 (Rawcliffe 1958, Campbell 1960). It was generally agreed that large sections of some counties were still missed. The census indicated a swan population in the region of 17,800-19,200. By making allowances for the areas not covered, however, a figure of 19,000-21,600 seems more likely (Ogilvie 1981).

Since some people, especially anglers and farmers, were worried that swan numbers were increasing rapidly, a partial census, restricted to 26 counties in England and Wales, was carried out in 1961, largely by aerial survey (Ogilvie 1972). This gave a figure for these areas of 12,000 swans, almost exactly the same total as found in the 1955-56 survey.

The 1978 survey was also a partial one. During the years 1968 to 1972, the British Trust for Ornithology had made a survey of all British breeding bird species, plotting their presence in each 10-km square of the National Grid. Roughly half the squares known to contain swans during this survey were re-surveyed in 1978. The results suggested that the total population of Mute Swans was probably about 17,630, a decline of 12-18 per cent since 1955 (Ogilvie 1981). The numbers of breeding pairs had declined from 3,550-4,000 in 1955 to 3,115 in 1978. There had, however, been a large decline in the numbers of flock birds (12,000-13,600 in 1955 to 9,700 in 1978). There were large regional variations in the changes, the most marked being declines in England and Wales and large increases in Scotland.

The latest census was carried out in 1983; this covered a larger area of Britain than the 1978 census, but again not the whole country. The results showed virtually no change since 1978 in the numbers of breeding pairs, but an increase in the numbers of non-breeders. The estimated totals were 3,150 pairs and 12,600 other swans, an increase of 7 per cent over 1978.

Another way of trying to count the swan population has been to use the figures from the Wildfowl Trust's monthly wildfowl counts. These counts have been aimed mainly at counting ducks and they tend to concentrate on the larger stretches of water and ignore the rivers and streams. Hence such counts are biased towards counting the flock birds and tend to miss the breeding pairs. The results of these counts are shown in Figure 3.1. They show a somewhat similar pattern to the census results, with numbers having decreased since the mid 1950s. The large decline in 1962/63 was almost certainly the result of high mortality during that very cold winter, since there was a fairly rapid partial recovery, but movement away from some areas may have made the decline appear more marked than it actually was.

Interpretation of these figures has led to considerable disputes. In particular, people working on swans in central England, where there have been marked declines, have been baffled as to why national censuses do not show numbers to be falling sharply. The main difficulties are that production of national figures of this sort can be quite misleading when, as is clearly the case with the Mute Swan, there are large differences between different areas of Britain. One of these differences can be seen between England and Scotland, numbers in the latter country having increased while in many areas of England they have decreased. Even this pattern may now have changed: quite large increases seem still to be taking place in northern Scotland, but the populations in some lowland areas have declined in recent years (Brown and Brown 1984, 1985).

Figure 3.1: Annual index of Mute Swan numbers in Britain, 1956 to 1985. This shows the numbers of birds, based on counts made for the Wildfowl Trust, in January each year. January 1971 was taken as the base line (and scored as 100). Note the large decline in the severe winter of 1963.

Data by courtesy of Dr M.A. Ogilvie

Another complication is that distributions within counties may be changing. For example, in certain areas such as Norfolk where there have been considerable problems with lead poisoning, numbers have not fallen so much as some would have predicted. This may be partly because of the very active Swan Rescue Service, but there have also been considerable shifts of distribution, with lower numbers on the rivers and lakes and increases in the birds on estuaries. To some extent at least, this shift indicates a drop in numbers of breeding pairs and an increase in flock birds and, if such a shift continued, one would expect numbers to fall in the long term.

Comparing the 1978 and 1983 censuses, there are marked regional effects of this sort. For example, if we compare those counties for which both censuses are thought to be more or less complete, the Mute Swans in coastal counties are faring much better than those in central England. There are 12 'central England' counties with complete coverage in both years (Nottinghamshire, Warwickshire, Huntingdonshire, Herefordshire,

Worcestershire, Gloucestershire, Oxfordshire, Berkshire, Buckingham-shire, Bedfordshire, Hertfordshire and Surrey). The two counts for these counties gave 2,882 and 2,581 for 1978 and 1983 respectively, a further drop in numbers of just over 10 per cent in five years. In contrast, the Fen and coastal counties of Lincolnshire, Cambridgeshire, Norfolk, Suffolk, Essex, Kent, Sussex, Hampshire, Dorset, Devon and Cornwall had combined totals of 5,455 and 6,755 swans in the two censuses, an increase of 23 per cent.

Plate 9. Reading in Berkshire has the largest flock of swans on the River Thames, but, even so, there are seldom more than 40 swans to be found at Caversham Bridge

Apart from the Thames population, there is only one other area where the breeding numbers of Mute Swans have been counted consistently over a longish period of years. This is the area which we refer to as the Midland study area. This study has been carried out mainly by A.E. Coleman, who has generously let us have his results. The numbers of breeding pairs of swans from 1961 to 1985 are shown in Figure 3.2. There has been a marked decline, mainly since the early 1970s. This pattern matches quite well what has happened on the Thames (see Figure 3.3, page 51). On the River Avon (Hardman and Cooper 1980), the Mute Swan has also declined seriously, from a total of 30 breeding pairs in 1964 to only some 10 pairs in 1984. The decline in non-breeders has been even more marked: the moulting flock in Stratford, up to almost 70 birds in the late 1960s, has now virtually disappeared.

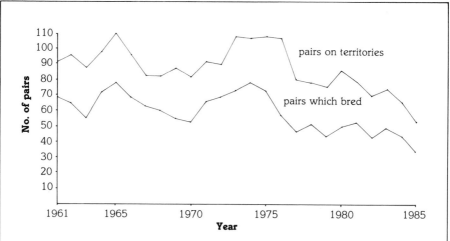

Figure 3.2: The numbers of territorial pairs of Mute Swans (upper line) and the numbers of pairs which bred (lower line) each year in the Midlands study area.

Data by courtesy of A.E. Coleman

The reasons for these declines are complex and to some extent disputed. We defer discussion of this subject until after we have discussed the numbers on the Thames.

The Thames Population

The Thames population of Mute Swans is the only one in Britain for which we have reliable records of numbers for any length of time. We presume that swan-upping was undertaken by the Crown for many years before the Vintners and Dyers Companies (see Chapter 2) were given rights to the birds (in the late fifteenth century). Subsequently, all three bodies have been involved in the swan-upping. We have found continuous records only since 1733 and even these are incomplete in certain ways (see below). Better records are available from 1823 onwards.

These records give us a fairly good indication of how the Thames population of Mute Swans has changed over the last two-and-a-half centuries or so, and how it was managed. Unfortunately, we have to say 'fairly good' because the records are not so good as we should have liked. We might have expected that all three bodies would have kept reasonably good records of these occasions. We have failed, however, to find any consistent records kept by the Crown's Swan Keeper. We have kindly been given access to the correspondence between HM Swan Keeper and the Lord Chamberlain's Office, and this has provided useful background information on a number of matters dealing with how the swans were looked after (this aspect is discussed at the end of this chapter). However, we have found no year-by-year records of the numbers of birds rounded up at swan-upping.

The Vintners' Records, 1733-1826

The earliest records we have are those of the Vintners Company from 1733 to 1826. There are, however, some problems with interpreting these. In the records from 1827 onwards (and in the Dyers' records from 1823 onwards), the catch is divided into swans and cygnets. If one takes the figures for one year, for example 1834, the totals of adults and cygnets (299 and 126 respectively) add up to more than the number of white birds caught the following year (315 in 1835). One would, of course, expect this: since virtually all the swans were pinioned, an increase in white birds could come about only through good survival of the cygnets of the previous year adding to the total of white birds which also survived to the following year. Conforming with this suggestion, in the run of figures from 1823 onwards the number of white birds in any year is practically never greater than the sum of white birds plus cygnets in the previous year.

The Vintners' records from 1733 to 1826 do not divide the birds in this way. There are, however, many instances where one year's total is larger than that of the previous year. We thought at one time that the records might have been of white birds only and that for some reason the cygnets had been excluded. This is not the case in the years 1823, 1825 and 1826, for which we have records from both the Vintners and the Dyers, the latter subdivided into swans and cygnets; in these years the Dyers' total and the Vintners' figures are almost identical. We are at a loss to explain why the Vintners' records show so many increases between one year and the next, but it does seem to cast some doubt on the accuracy of the records.

The Vintners' and Dyers' Records since 1823

Since 1823, annual records have been kept by the two livery companies, with the cygnets recorded separately. Here, again, we are in some difficulty in that the two sets of records do not always agree. Up to about 1900, the numbers of cygnets recorded at swan-upping agree very closely. From then on, until about 1960, there are quite large discrepancies in the totals recorded, with the Vintners registering larger totals in almost all years; the extreme was in 1922, when the Vintners recorded 275 cygnets compared with the Dyers' total of 125, a twofold difference! We have been unable to discover with certainty how such large discrepancies came about, but the likely explanation seems to be that the Vintners enthusiastically counted a lot of swans off the normal stretch of Thames (which went only up to Henley). It is clear that in a number of the years in question swans were upped in a wide range of places after swan-upping. For example, in 1925, the King's Swan Keeper, Turk, wrote to the Lord Chamberlain's Office: 'there are a few birds in outlying districts still to be pinioned; also those between Reading and Henley'. In 1937, Turk wrote: 'the number of cygnets pinioned for His Majesty was 108 from London to Tilehurst' (upstream of Reading).

In 1938, there were plans to extend swan-upping as far as Pangbourne, though apparently they got only as far upstream as Malpledurham, a few miles upstream of Tilehurst. In addition, it is apparent that they were going back along the river at later dates to find extra broods. For example, in a letter to the Lord Chamberlain's Office in 1925, Turk wrote: 'birds not caught at swan-upping (ie. those up side-streams etc.) are usually dealt with after Swan Upping, sometime during August and early September'.

We are inclined to believe that the Dyers' records give the most accurate account of the numbers of swans on the River Thames itself from London to Henley. Each year, after swan-upping, the Dyers' records are meticulously transferred from field notebooks to beautiful, leather-bound volumes. While beauty is, of course, no guarantee of accuracy, the Dyers' records provide a detailed account of swan-upping with the exact positions of each brood and all the other birds found. Hence, we can at least be sure that the birds recorded did actually come from the correct stretch of river and that only the Thames from London to Henley was included. Therefore, we tend to believe that these books accurately record the number of Mute Swans encountered on this stretch of the river. Even these books, however, are not wholly internally consistent, since the non-breeding birds are not always included in the records; in some years, only the pairs with their broods are listed. For this reason, most of what we have to say about these numbers is restricted to the breeding pairs and their cygnets. Since the marking of the new cohort of cygnets is the main aim of swan-upping, it does seem likely that this part of the story should be the most accurately recorded.

Population Trends

If we accept the Vintners' figures for the early period as being at least a guide to the numbers, we can see that there have been several major changes in numbers of swans present on the Thames since the beginning of the eighteenth century (Figure 3.3). Numbers were very low in the earliest years, but built up fairly steadily until there were around 700 in the late 1750s. Thereafter they gradually fell away again until, towards the end of the century, they were fluctuating around the 300 mark. Then, numbers declined even further, falling to only 84 in 1801 and 80, the lowest ever recorded, in 1805. After that they increased again to another peak (of almost 600 white birds) in the late 1850s, before falling away again rather gradually to a low of just over 200 white birds in 1905. This was followed by a steady increase, until once again there were getting on for 500 white birds by the 1930s; numbers then levelled off slightly for a few years and then continued to rise until they peaked at just over 1,300 in 1964. After that, they declined steadily. At the time of writing, the number of Mute Swans on the Thames from London to Henley, the stretch orginally covered for swan-upping, is now reduced to about 120 white birds.

The numbers of pairs with cygnets on the river at swan-upping are shown in Figure 3.4. This shows a slightly different pattern from that for the total numbers. Numbers of breeding pairs were low in the 1820s, but fairly stable from then until the 1920s, when they started to increase steadily, reaching their highest level in the 1950s. After that, the numbers of pairs, like the overall numbers, started to decline until, at the time of writing, they are lower than at any point since 1820.

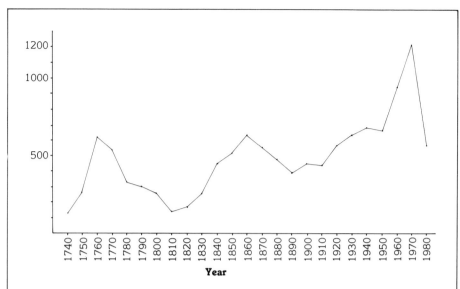

Figure 3.3: Average numbers of Mute Swans on the River Thames, London to Henley, at swan-upping. Each point is the average of the numbers during the previous decade. The highest numbers recorded were 1,309 in 1964. The decline during the 1970s was more rapid than is apparent from such an average figure; there were 1,046 in 1971 and only 114 in 1980.

Data by courtesy of the Vintners Company

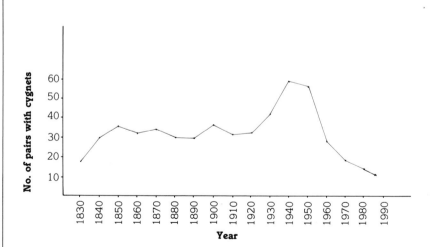

Figure 3.4: The average numbers of families of Mute Swans on the River Thames, from London to Henley, at swan-upping. Each point shows the average number of broods during a ten-year period, i.e. the point for 1900 is the average for the years 1891-1900. The last point is based on the years 1981-85.

Data from the Dyers Company records

Reason for the Changes

We have no idea why most of the earlier changes in numbers occurred. The largest ones were the increases which took place during the early part of this century. These started in the early 1900s, and by the early 1920s the increase was becoming marked and some people were starting to complain that there were too many swans. One of the most notable factors of this period of increase is that there were large numbers of flyers — birds coming in onto the Thames from elsewhere. Some of these became established breeders on the river. It is even more impressive that this increase in the swans was occurring against a background of attempts to curb their numbers. During the late 1920s and throughout the 1930s, control measures were being taken. The fact that the population continued to increase despite culls of these proportions shows how well the swans were doing.

What was the cause of this increase? There may have been a number of different factors involved. There was a growing interest in wildlife and, in addition, strenuous attempts were being made to clean up the river, especially by preventing oil from being spilled. Oil spillages seem to have been widespread earlier and from time to time led to the deaths of many swans. For example, in June 1930 it was claimed, in a letter to the Lord Chamberlain's Office, that some 40 swans at Kew Bridge were in poor condition; the writer of the letter noted that fish had disappeared from this stretch about two years previously, 'killed by the oil and grease of motor engines'. Even as late as the 1940s, this seems to have been a serious problem. In October 1942, Turk noted that (because of fuel rationing during the war) 'the absence of petrol boats on the river has enabled the birds to keep clean and free from oil'.

An unusual source of pollution was oil bombs dropped over London during the Blitz. When these fell on the water they caused wide-scale damage to the swans. In November 1940, the Comptroller at the Lord Chamberlain's Office wrote in answer to an enquiry: 'during the present month upwards of 70 birds have been caught up and destroyed, this being the only humane thing to do'. It looks as if the bombing more or less exterminated swans in the central London area at that time, there being only four at Hammersmith in November of 1940. Further, the Lower Thames was much fouled at this time from general pollution, not just oil. Although conditions were worst on the lower reaches, they were pretty bad throughout London and indeed above it. It is only in the period from 1950 onwards that there have been marked signs of improvement.

The increase in some species of wildfowl on the Lower Thames has been shown to be the result of these clean-ups (Harrison and Grant 1976). It is interesting to note that these changes do not fit with the changes in swan numbers. The big increase in swans started well before the cleaning-up of the river and was almost certainly the result of things that were happening off the main river itself. By far the largest factor here seems to have been the creation of new habitats by the digging of gravel-pits. These produced a rash of new and highly suitable breeding sites where some of the 'surplus' flyers could go and breed. As now, the territorial parents on the gravel-pits chased off their young during the course of the winter and, in addition, the aquatic vegetation died down in midwinter with the result that even some of the adults had to move elsewhere; it was this multitude of young birds plus some of their parents that gathered on the Thames, adding to the already successful local population.

At this time, all the swans (and their cygnets) which were caught at swan-upping were pinioned. This was, of course, done historically so that the birds would not fly away and could be caught up again when wanted. Pinioning provides us with a bit of interesting information, as any bird which was caught at swan-upping and which was not pinioned had obviously come on to the river since the previous year. During the increase in the 1930s, the Swan Keeper was reporting to the Lord Chamberlain's Office that there were more and more flyers. Hence, during the years when the population was expanding, an increasing number of swans were coming on to the Thames from elsewhere.

Since swan-upping seems to have gradually died out in most areas by about the middle of the last century, the sudden increase in the numbers of flyers in the 1920s and 1930s cannot have been the direct result of people stopping pinioning elsewhere. It seems likely that the swans were moving in from the surrounding network of rivers. Presumably, since the flyers were coming in increasing numbers, the populations in other areas, such as the tributaries, were also increasing steadily. Almost certainly, the steady increase in gravel-pits and other ponds in the Thames Valley played a major part in this growth in the number of flyers that were coming onto the Thames.

These new gravel-pits provided good habitats for several other species of waterbirds. Great Crested Grebes, *Podiceps cristatus*, and Tufted Ducks, *Aythya fuligula*, also flourished on these waters and have increased in numbers (Ogilvie 1986). Slightly more recently, there have also been enormous increases in Canada Geese, *Branta canadensis*. In Nottinghamshire, these have been attributed to changes in agriculture which have favoured the Canada Geese, as well as to the provision of suitable breeding areas in the form of gravel-pits (Parkin and McMeeking 1985). In the London area, the Canada Goose populations did not 'take off' until into the 1930s (Blurton Jones 1956), whereas the population of Mute Swans on the Lower Thames had clearly started to increase well before then. The reason why the dramatic increase in geese did not occur until later was possibly that there were only very small numbers present in the early part of this century (they were introduced from North America); for a long time they were largely confined to parks, and do not seem to have really started to establish large populations in the wild until the 1930s or even later in some areas. The increase in Canada Geese is causing conservationists some concern and we shall return to this problem at the end of this book.

The Decline

Suddenly, this healthy, burgeoning, post-war population of Mute Swans checked and started to decline. In the space of some 25 years, it plummeted from the highest recorded numbers to the lowest. We know that this was not just a simple result of a general deterioration in the habitat; not only was the river being cleaned up, but, as just mentioned, several other waterbird species — the Tufted Duck, Great Crested Grebe and Canada Goose — were increasing while the Mute Swan declined.

Although again the most extensive data are for the Thames, we know that what happened to the Thames swans happened in other places, such as in the Midlands and on the Avon at Stratford. Stratford is in the constituency of Dennis Howell, then Minister of State at the Department of the Environment, and it was his questioning that prompted the original enquiry by the Nature Conservancy Council and some of the investigations discussed later (Chapter 7).

The exact moment when the problem became serious is difficult to pinpoint, though it does seem to have been reasonably synchronous in these different areas. Also, with the wisdom of hindsight, there were warning signs on the Thames for some time before anyone fully appreciated that there was a problem. The reason for this is that people continued to see large numbers of swans on the Thames until the late 1960s, but this was probably because of continued high immigration of flyers. The breeding success of the Thames birds had already started to decline. In a letter to the Lord Chamberlain dated 22 December 1964, Captain Turk wrote: 'The Companies' Swan Markers and I were surprised that more nesting birds were not found ... but it was noticeable that the Lower Reaches, below Staines, are very short of young birds. The Companies are quite concerned about this.' In another letter (9 December 1969), Captain Turk reported that 'The number of birds caught was disappointing. Only fourteen broods, comprising thirty-nine cygnets ...'

This difference is apparent in Figures 3.3 and 3.4; the start of the decline in the numbers of breeding pairs preceded that for the overall numbers by about a decade. In view of what was happening to the total numbers prior to the decline and what we see happening to the population today (see page 44), it looks very much as if the flyers were still arriving on the Thames in sufficient numbers to mask what would have been a clear decline had the Thames been isolated from swans in other areas.

As already mentioned, the decline has been most marked in inland counties from southern England up to the north Midlands, but other areas such as Yorkshire and Lancashire also seem to have lost large numbers of their Mute Swans in the last 20 years. With only poor knowledge of the numbers in most of these areas, at least until the first national census was attempted in 1955, it is hard to be confident of the exact picture. One point, however, does seem worth stressing: the decline in swan numbers happened fairly suddenly to a population that had hitherto been increasing sharply. Further, one might have predicted that the population would have gone on increasing because its habitat was being expanded. This is most dramatically shown in the data produced by Ogilvie (1986), who compares the changes in swan numbers with those of Great Crested Grebes and Tufted Ducks, two other species which have benefited by the increase in gravel-pits. Why did the Mute Swan numbers not behave like those of the grebe and the duck and indeed the Canada Goose? Something very adverse to its survival must have happened to have caused this dramatic change. The reason for this is discussed in Chapter 7.

The Management of the Thames Swans

Introduction

In the previous sections we have discussed the numbers of Mute Swans on the River Thames, the information being based largely on the records of the Vintners and Dyers Companies. This population has obviously been heavily managed for many centuries and in this section we outline the history of that management since the beginning of the present century. The swans are still 'upped' every summer on behalf of the Crown and the two livery companies, and the cygnets are marked, though the birds are no longer pinioned.

Care for the Thames Swans

The original aim of the swan-upping was, of course, to provide a stock of birds for the table. There do not seem to be records of how many were taken for this purpose each year. The tradition seems, however, to have been largely curtailed about 1909, when King Edward VII commanded that no more cygnets should be fattened and killed. At that time, 'the practice was disposing of about 30 per year'. This is confirmed in a letter from the Lord Chamberlain's Office, dated 4 October 1909, in reply to a request from a somewhat optimistic subject for two cygnets for Christmas:

> 'I have to let you know that an order was very recently given that no further birds were to be killed for this purpose.'

This decision can have referred only to the Crown's share of the birds, since the Vintners and Dyers certainly had cygnet at their annual Swan Dinners for some time after that. This is borne out in a letter from Turk, the King's Swan Keeper, to the Lord Chamberlain in December 1963, when, after an exceptionally hard winter, the swans did not raise many young. Turk noted that the Vintners and Dyers 'were having trouble getting enough for their feasts'.

Since the decision by the King to stop taking swans for eating was made at a time (November 1909) when there were already complaints about there being too many swans in certain areas (the November meeting was told that there were 540 swans on the Thames at that time), there was a worry that the population might increase even further and it was resolved to give away as many as possible to private waters; there was even a move to approach Lord Ilchester (the owner of Abbotsbury), since he 'had ample accommodation for more'. At the same time, there was a suggestion that the flyers should not be pinioned and that some of the Thames cygnets should also be left unpinioned. This was presumably in the hopes that they would fly away. The suggestion was, however, rejected for fear of people starting to shoot them.

Duties of HM Swan Keeper

Many of the original duties of HM Swan Keeper have been described in Chapter 2. Over recent years, with the cessation of having to run the complex system of swan-marking throughout the country, the duties have been largely confined to the River Thames and have changed somewhat, though basically the holder of the position is still responsible for all aspects of the welfare and management of the Thames swans. Often these duties result in his being called out to deal with a variety of problems, from the most common of dealing with sick and injured swans to the more bizarre. Increasingly in the records there are comments to the effect than many of the injuries were to flyers, who are obviously more prone to damage themselves in collisions than are pinioned birds.

Many people found some reason for complaining about the swans. The complaints included those (usually in summer, when the birds were caring for their young) about dangerous swans. For example:

L.M. Deakin (July 1913)

'I wish to call your attention to the savage condition of one of the swans frequenting the church backwater at Wargrave which I consider a danger to the public ... It has already attacked one or two people I know and when I was out again this morning, we had to keep it off with the sculls and boat hook.'

Catherine Grice (July 1921)

'We get no peace day or night from him ... in every way it is most distressing ... and it would be a courtesy on your part to have the big tryannerus [sic] beast destroyed.'

Others claimed that they were suffering damage. For example:

W.G. Stoneham (April 1906)

'I have again been asked by the poor tenement holders at Dorney-Lake-End to ask your assistance. One of the swans has returned and is preventing their ducks using the "rights" "of Common" which is a serious matter at breeding time.'

G. Stanley (early 1915) made a claim for £9.10s for damage by swans to a watercress bed (he got about a third of this, so tried again the following year and was less successful!). Caversham Constitutional Club (June 1931) made an original, but unsuccessful claim: 'swan crashed onto roof, broke glass light which wrecked new cloth on billiard table. Any recompense?'

Recompense was normally denied, since the Crown had by then ceased to lay any claim to flyers, regarding them as outside its jurisdiction. For example, in 1931, Turk wrote in a letter that 'the owners of the swans on the Thames do not hold themselves responsible for any damage which may be occasioned by swans flying; our swans are pinioned ...' He was equally clear to a car owner whose windscreen was shattered when the car was in collison with a flying swan; free-flying swans were not his responsibility and the car owner must claim on his insurance.

Flying swans were increasingly a problem to people who had power cables or telephone wires across rivers (to say nothing of the problem these wires were, and still are, for the birds). The problem multiplied, doubtless because of the increasing numbers of wires as well as the increasing numbers of swans. Clearly, the pinioned birds were not responsible! In 1934, circulars were sent to all the Councils along the river about cutting down the numbers of swans and the need to pinion them; a leaflet on how to pinion the birds was included with the letter.

Increasingly, too, there were notes to the effect that the Swan Keeper was having to deal with birds injured by fishing hooks. Although there do not appear to be any good records of the numbers of anglers on the Thames, if the number of fishing hooks in swans is anything to go by there seems to have been a fairly large increase in angling in the late 1950s, when Turk reported being called out on several occasions.

Another duty that the Swan Keeper had (and still has) was to catch up all the swans on the Henley reach for about a fortnight each year, so as to avoid problems between the swans and the boats during the Henley Regatta. This task dates back to 1894, when there were two collisions between racing boats and swans and the Regatta Committee asked the Lord Chamberlain's Office to do this, agreeing to pay the cost of the operation. Similar removals have taken place on other stretches during regattas, for example at Marlow and Staines, but not over so long a period of years. In 1908, the birds were kept off the river for a much longer period because the Olympics were also staged at Henley.

Care of the Birds in Winter

Another problem that clearly took up a lot of time and was the cause of considerable concern was the care of the swans in the winter. Partly as the result of a number of hard winters, and perhaps also because the birds were pinioned and so could not wander afield, there were a number of bitter complaints about the condition of many of the swans during harsh winters. Some of the complainants pointed out that pinioning was the root cause of the problem.

Two actions were taken over this. First, with the help of the Thames Conservancy, it was agreed that the lock-keepers would feed the birds regularly during the winter. It is not clear for how long this was done, but table 3.1 lists the locks where food was provided during the winter of 1907/08 and the numbers of swans that were attending each of the feeders. The total fed during this winter seems somewhat at odds with the statement made during January of that year that there were about 400 swans to be fed; Turk wrote to the Lord Chamberlain to this effect, pointing out that only about one-third of the birds seemed to use these feeders.

The lock-keepers were paid five shillings per month for doing this and the food was delivered by barge. It was estimated that each swan needed daily 1.5 lb (0.7 kg) of bread, 1 lb (0.45 kg) of oats and some greens, the total cost of the operation (including labour and food) being about £133. In the following winter, as a result of these experiences, it was also decided to split up the troughs in which the birds were fed in order to reduce the problems of a dominant swan preventing the others from getting at the food.

The date at which feeding was to start was a matter for some debate. In 1909, the Swan Keeper (Abnett) was supposed to have arranged for feeding to start on 15 December, but he could not get a barge in time to distribute the food. There were complaints of hungry swans wandering around and the Lord Chamberlain sent Abnett a sharp note about it. In 1913, Abnett (who did not seem to get on well with the Lord Chamberlain, Sir Douglas Dewar) got it wrong again when he asked, on 14 December, if he should start feeding the swans. The reply said, somewhat acidly, 'Sir Douglas Dewar wishes me to say that, as he was cutting his grass yesterday, he does not think it necessary to start feeding the swans yet.'

Table 3.1: Numbers of Mute Swans fed at different locks by the lock-keepers and ferrymen in 1907

Richmond	10
Kingston	25
Hampton	9
Sunbury	4
Shepperton	10
Chertsey	4
Penton Hook	22
Bell Weir	14
Old Windsor	6
Romney	32
Boveney	4
Bray	22
Boulters	6
Cookham Ferry	4
Cookham Lock	4
Spade Oak Ferry	9
Marlow	4
Temple	2
Hurley	2
Aston Ferry	6
Hambledon	6
Marsh	3
Total	208

The habit of feeding the swans in winter ceased about 1922, partly as a result of the doubts expressed about its efficacy and partly because of the rising costs (it cost £327.1s.4d in 1918/19). Nevertheless, something had to be done for the birds in winter and so it was agreed that, in periods of very prolonged frosts, all the swans should be rounded up and kept off the river until conditions improved. In 1927, all the birds were taken up around 19 December and not released until 17 January 1928. In 1929, Turk took up the swans about 13 February and released them again on 23 March (there were 312 Crown birds; included in the swans taken up were about 100 flyers, and it is not clear whether these were included in, or additional to, the 312). Since there had been complaints of too many swans in Windsor in particular, some 60 or so, presumably flyers, were removed from Windsor and Medmenham and not

Plate 10. Today's lock-keepers are still concerned about the Mute Swan. This cygnet had been caught up in discarded fishing line

returned 'to that district'; presumably they were pinioned and released elsewhere, but, in view of the fact that some swans were later destroyed, this may have been the fate of these birds too.

The swans were taken up again on 21 December 1938 (no number is given, but they were collected from as far upstream as Oxford) and released during the period 9-11 January 1939 (the total cost being £209). Again, many of the flyers were not released, being 'disposed of' (page 62). The birds were taken to a variety of riverside places where they could be kept and looked after, the person looking after them being paid for his time. Since the swans were not marked at this time, one wonders what happened to the pairs. Presumably, the birds from one stretch of river were held together and released again on the same stretch. If this did not always happen, however, then there would be a fair chance that the pairs would have been split up and this might well have affected how many pairs bred.

The swans do not seem to have been removed from the river after 1938/39. There was a belief that they should again be removed in the hard winter of 1939/40, but it was wartime and people did not feel justified in doing so. In fact, the birds seem to have managed reasonably well for themselves in spite of the prolonged cold period that winter. It was noted that the swans on the lower reaches suffered more than those higher up, presumably because areas where they could graze were already much more restricted.

Control of Numbers

The increase in swan numbers seems to have been a subject of concern for some years. In 1925, the suggestion was made that the number of eggs in the nests should be reduced in an attempt to control the population. This suggestion was not accepted at the time, but it was in the following year. The plan was to visit as many of the nests as possible and to reduce the number of eggs to two. It is clear from the Dyers' records (in which the size of broods was recorded) that this was fairly effective and was carried out every year from 1926 to 1948 inclusive. There appears to have been some objection by the nesters (persons who had a nest on their land, and who guarded it and were rewarded for their pains if the nest was successful), presumably since they lost money because the number of young hatching was reduced. This seems to have been overcome by paying them for the eggs removed.

There are a number of letters over the years from Captain Turk, the King's Swan Keeper, to the Lord Chamberlain, reporting on the egg removals. For example, on 29 May 1926, after a four-day trip, Turk wrote 'we have removed a proportion of the eggs'; and, after swan-upping in the same summer, 'taking away of eggs in the spring has proved successful; it has reduced the cygnets by about one third compared with last year' (it should have been by almost two-thirds if they had found all the nests). In a further letter of 15 November of the same year, he stated: '... the number of eggs taken that I have paid the nesters for is 57 and the cygnets number 119 whereas last year there were 175 cygnets all told. This is taking into account all birds pinioned during Swan Upping and since. These are Crown birds only.' (According to the Vintners' records, only 75 cygnets were marked for the Crown during swan-upping itself in 1926 and 127 in the previous year.)

In 1927, Turk reported that he had visited all the nests on the stretch from Mapledurham to Richmond and reduced the clutches to two, though he left clutches of only one on the Reading stretch 'as there are great numbers of birds there'. In 1928, he again visited nests from Mapledurham to Putney and removed 150 eggs. Assuming that an average clutch of six eggs was being reduced to just two, i.e. that an average of about four eggs was being taken from each nest, this implies that close to 40 nests were being found; this tallies reasonably well with the Dyers' records for that year, which record that there were 33 broods of two between London and Henley (a few of which might have been natural).

In 1929, Turk reported: '... when we removed just over 150 eggs which has this year been a great success keeping down the numbers to be hatched'. Again, in 1930: 'I have visited the nests from Pangbourne down to Putney and have taken out the usual eggs leaving two in most nests, but where there were a number of nests only one ... the number taken was about 150 eggs.' In 1930, Turk also recorded that there were greater numbers that could fly, which was 'getting fairly serious'. In 1933, Turk reported that he 'took out a proportion of the eggs as usual' and that there were 'a few more cygnets than last year, but a good drop compared with '31.'

By 1934, with numbers showing no signs of diminishing and with a rash of complaints, especially about flyers breaking overhead cables, even more drastic steps were decided upon. Firstly, clutches from Oxford downwards were reduced, not just those from Reading as had been the case hitherto. Turk reported: 'eggs collected Oxford to Putney. Nests were plentiful.'

There are no records of the totals of eggs removed on this longer stretch of river, but by 1939 it was reported that there were fewer swans than usual. This seems, however, to have been only partly due to the removal of eggs, since additional measures were now in force. The reduction was at least partly 'due to our treatment of them in the winter'. This relates to the culling of flyers. This, it seems, had been done on occasion since the late 1920s, but was not carried out on a large scale until 1934, after the meeting at which it was decided to extend the taking of eggs up to Oxford. In addition, there was to be an annual round-up 'to remove redundant birds'. At this meeting, it was also decided that riparian councils were to be encouraged to pinion the flyers, this having been done to 30 birds at Windsor in the previous year to prevent complaints about their breaking telephone wires.

Culling of swans, presumably almost always flyers, is not well documented. The first records we have found are for 1929, when about 65 birds were removed. In November 1933, 83 were removed from between Iffley Lock and Folly Bridge (Oxford), but a further 50 came in there within a month; these were apparently also removed. A largish number were probably also removed from Reading in the same winter. In 1934, after the decision to implement a regular winter cull as part of the control policy, 54 swans were removed from Oxford, 35 from

Windsor, 70 from Reading, 36 from Staines and 70 from Hammersmith: a total of 265. In 1935, 76 were removed from Oxford. In 1937, 75 were removed from Oxford, 30 from Reading, 32 from Windsor and 27 from Staines: a total of 164, all of which were flyers. In November 1938, 25 were removed from Windsor, 63 from Reading, 72 from Oxford and 25 from Staines: a total of 185 birds. The picture is a bit complicated in this last year, because many birds were taken up and cared for during a cold spell in December, after which Turk reported 'I disposed of 157 birds which was a fairly large undertaking'. It seems as if the 157 were additional to the 185 removed in the previous month, in which case the total cull on the river that year was 342.

We found no records of culls continuing into the war period or after it, although perhaps rationing encouraged illegal taking of both eggs and birds. Removal of eggs, however, went on during and after the war. In May 1941, Turk wrote to the Lord Chamberlain's Office: 'took away eggs as usual'. In 1959, Turk notes 'I also took less eggs this year than in those years stated' (1956-58). The last record we have found is for 1961, when Turk wrote to the Lord Chamberlain's Office that he 'took very few eggs again as we didn't seem to have too many nests and the piniomed birds appear to be getting short'.

There are some puzzles about these later records. The Dyers' records show no signs that many nests were reduced to two eggs after 1948, though they relate to swan-upping and so refer only to broods from London to Henley. Their records show the following numbers of broods of two: 1942, 70; 1943, 50; 1944, 44; 1945, 46; 1946, 57; 1947, 32; 1948, 14; 1949, 10; 1950, 8; 1951, 4. There are no signs from these figures that many broods were reduced to two in any subsequent year except perhaps in 1957, when 14 broods of two were upped.

There are two aspects of all these records which we have not been able to understand. The first concerns the taking of eggs so as to reduce the clutches to two. In Turk's statements to the Lord Chamberlain's Office, he implies that this has the effect of reducing the number of young by about a third. This would seem to be reasonable since it would be most unlikely that, in a four-day trip down the river (the total time spent), they would find all the nests; almost certainly, a goodly number up small side creeks would be missed. Hence the theoretical reduction by two-thirds would be most unlikely to be achieved. The Dyers' records, however, paint a very different picture. For example, these give 303 broods for the five years 1938 to 1942, all but two of which were of just two cygnets! This implies fantastically efficient nest-finding, or perhaps additional culling at swan-upping. Further, there were no broods of one at all in these years. This seems difficult to understand in view of the fact that, unless the eggs were carefully floated (to see which ones were developing) before any were removed, normal hatching failure would have resulted in quite a number (roughly one in ten: see page 71) of clutches of two ending up as broods of one in such a large sample. Further, what happened to the nests which were reduced to one egg?

Another point which we do not understand concerns the relationship between the counts at swan-upping and the flyers. Both the Vintners' and the Dyers' records carefully divide all the white birds recorded at swan-upping according to whether they belonged to the Crown or to one or other of the two Companies (they could be told by the number of nicks in the bill: see page 22). This implies that all the birds were caught up and the marks on their bills examined. Since they were pinioned, this would have been perfectly possible, although rather laborious to do. The flyers, however, would not have had bill-marks, since, by definition, they would not have been caught and pinioned as cygnets. As all unmarked swans belonged to the Crown, the flyers might have been counted as Crown birds. It seems unlikely, however, that the flyers were counted, because they were trying to discourage, or even dispose of, them. We think that the birds attributed to the Crown at swan-upping must have been much the same as those of the two Companies: pinioned birds, with a high proportion of breeders among them.

We therefore presume that the large majority of the flyers were not on the Thames at swan-upping, but flew in during the winter when their food supplies elsewhere started to diminish. This would fit with the observation for 1933, given above, that a stretch of river at Oxford, having been cleared in November, held a further 50 flyers on it in December. Hence we suggest that the majority of the flyers were additional to, and not part of, the Thames counts made at swan-upping. This point has not, to our knowledge, been made before in relation to the Thames counts and, if true, emphasises the very large numbers of swans that there must have been in the Thames Valley at that time.

CHAPTER

4

Life-History Studies

Introduction

The number of Mute Swans on the River Thames has fluctuated during the last 250 years, culminating in a marked decline during the last 25 years. Although there are no comparable censuses of swans in other parts of the country, this decline has been mirrored by declines on other lowland rivers.

In this chapter we examine the population dynamics of the Mute Swan and look at the ways in which what we know can be used to understand the changes which take place in the numbers of swans. In order to do this, we need to describe the pattern of birth, life and death in swans, the so-called life-table. However, one needs to be careful. The fact that swan populations are increasing in parts of Scotland and decreasing in central England should put one on one's guard; a simple, single life-table cannot be appropriate countrywide. Unfortunately, we have detailed studies of only four Mute Swan populations in Britain, and these do not allow us to explain adequately the differences between areas. Worse still in a way, the two most detailed studies, those around Oxford and in the Midlands, are basically in rather similar habitats. While this is good in the sense that the information from the two studies is reassuringly similar, giving us some confidence in our findings, it is a pity in the sense that we need more information about what happens in other habitats. The other two detailed studies come from the Hebrides and from the colony at Abbotsbury on the Fleet in Dorset. As we shall see, the results from these two areas are quite different from those in Oxford and the Midlands. In some, but not all, respects, however, these other two areas are also similar to each other. The Hebridean population seems to be the most 'natural'. Unfortunately, this study was made for only five years, in two of which (1978/79 and 1981/82) there were very severe winters; these probably led to an unusually high number of birds dying, so that the observed survival rates may not be typical of a normal run of years.

We provide here a number of sets of data from these studies. As mentioned in the Preface, the sources of these data can be obtained from the bibliography under the following authors: 1) Oxford: Bacon, Birkhead, Perrins, Reynolds. 2) Midlands: Coleman, Minton. 3) Hebrides: Spray. 4) Abbotsbury: Ogilvie, Perrins.

Population Structure

For our purposes here, the changes in numbers that have occurred over the years — and that are still occurring — can all be linked with changes in either the birth rate or the death rate of the birds. Basically, if a population remains stable, the number of deaths within that population is balanced by the number of births. It is often easier to say that, in a stable population, the number of eggs which hatch and produce young which survive to reach breeding age must equal the number of breeding adults which die. In this chapter, we look at what is known about these birth rates and death rates.

Locally, changes in numbers can, of course, also result from emigration and/or immigration. Since we are dealing here with the entire population of Mute Swans in the British Isles, and since we know that movement in and out of Britain is very rare (page 13), we can ignore the rates of emigration and immigration on this scale. Indeed, since it is also rather rare for Mute Swans to move more than 100 km or so (page 14), we can to a large extent ignore many of the problems of emigration and immigration on an even smaller scale; for instance, the number of birds moving in and out of any one of Britain's main river systems is sufficiently small that this has, at most, very trivial effects on population changes. On a local scale, however, movement may play an important role in the life cycle of the birds and we shall return to this subject later.

Two other aspects of the life cycle of a bird may seriously affect the balance of numbers. These are the age at which the individuals start to breed, and how often they breed from then on. We shall deal with these two points first.

Age at First Breeding

The later in life at which the individuals start to breed, the greater the chance that they will die before they start breeding. We can see how important this is by looking at the figures in Table 4.5 (page 77). Here, out of each year's breeding attempt, an average of 0.43 young per pair survive to reach the age of four; 0.32 would survive to the age of five (assuming that they continued to have the 75 per cent survival rate found for immatures). In this particular study, an average of 0.36 cygnets per pair had to survive to breed if the population was to remain stable.

This would have been achieved if the birds had started to breed at four, but if they had not started to breed until the age of five the population could not have maintained itself. This is an oversimplified example in that we have assumed that all the figures are exactly right, but it does indicate the importance of knowing the age at which breeding commences in a population.

In practice, an accurate estimate of the age of first breeding is not easy to make, largely because there is considerable variation in the time at which the individual birds start. Some idea of this variation is given in Table 4.1. Some of the spread also arises from a difference between the sexes: male swans start to breed, on average, a little later than females.

Table 4.1: Age at which Mute Swans start breeding

Age of bird in years	% breeding at			
	Oxford	Radipole	Midlands(1)	Midlands(2)
2	—	3	3	12
3	10	21	47	31
4	37	58	82	47
5	53	71	97	68
6	71	83		

Note: The Oxford figures and those labelled Midlands(1) were collected in the 1960s when the population was still high; the other two sets in the 1970s, by which time the population had fallen markedly. Note particularly the change in age of first breeding between the two Midlands periods, with more birds starting to breed at two in the second period

Most of these studies show the same thing: a high proportion of the birds starting to breed at the ages of three or four. A very few birds, mostly females, first breed at the age of two. Others start much later, with one or two birds having been recorded in the non-breeding flocks for up to ten years without ever apparently attempting to breed. On average, the Oxford and Midlands birds tend to start breeding at the age of four, and this is the figure that we use in some estimates later in this chapter.

There are two other points of interest about these figures. Although the Oxford and Midlands studies indicate that breeding starts at about the same time, there is some evidence that the average age of first breeding has declined over the years, with a higher proportion of birds now breeding at the age of three than was the case at the beginning of the studies. This is not unexpected, since the populations are now much lower than they were in the 1960s and it should therefore be easier for aspiring breeders to find suitable vacant territories. Breeding at two has also been recorded under good conditions in captivity (Howard 1935).

The second point concerns the age of first breeding in the Hebridean Mute Swan population. Although, unfortunately, the study was not carried on long enough to establish the average age at which the birds start to breed, this must be later than in the other populations studied. During the Hebridean study, no birds (out of a possible 89) bred at the age of two. Similarly, no three-year-old birds (out of a possible 34) bred and, of 25 birds which reached the age of four during the study, only one bred.

Non-breeding

Before we can start looking at the breeding success of a population, we need to know how many pairs there are. This is not so easy as it sounds, even for so conspicuous a bird as a Mute Swan. This is because most studies of Mute Swans have reported a high proportion of pairs which are present and defending territories, but which do not breed. For example, in a survey of many English rivers, Eltringham (1963) recorded that about 20 per cent of the pairs did not appear to be nesting. Minton's (1968) more detailed Midlands study showed that about 30 per cent of the pairs did not breed in any one year.

As the female incubates, the male may sit patiently at her side

There are a number of reasons why certain individuals do not breed in a given year. Some, recorded as non-breeders, are doubtless birds that do breed, but fail at an early stage; in such cases, the observer just does not make enough visits to the site to record the nesting attempt during the brief period when it is happening. We simply do not know how frequent such occurrences are, but they are probably not very important in detailed studies, although they may be important in national censuses where only single visits are made to each territory.

In many cases, the birds no doubt really are non-breeders. There are two main reasons why pairs do not breed. First, as discussed later (page 88), young swans commonly pair and take up territory a year before breeding. Second, many birds that have bred successfully in one year,

Plate 11. This proud pen has an exceptionally large clutch of 11 eggs. The average clutch-size is about six eggs

but have lost their mate by the next season, may spend a year in the company of a new mate before breeding again. This may happen even if both members of the new pair are experienced breeders, not just if (as often happens) one of the new pair is a younger bird. In the Midlands study, there was a much higher proportion of non-breeding pairs after the very hard winter of early 1963. This was apparently a result of the unusually high number of adult birds which had lost mates in the winter and had paired up with new ones; possibly some established pairs, however, also failed to breed because they were in poor condition after the prolonged cold spell.

Clutch-size

The clutch-size of the Mute Swan has been measured in a number of studies (Table 4.2). There is remarkably little variation; clutches in almost all areas average in the region of 5.5-7 eggs and, although there are differences between years within the same area, the differences between areas seem to be fairly small. One exception to this is the colony of swans at Abbotsbury, where the average clutch-size is a little less than five eggs (Perrins and Ogilvie 1981). This figure might not be strictly comparable with those elsewhere, since daily visits are made to all the nests and, therefore, even clutches of one and two — which may last for only a very short time — are recorded. Even if we discount all the clutches of one or two eggs, however, the average clutch-size is only just over five eggs, and this is still lower than the average found elsewhere.

There are also other small variations in clutch-size. Clutches vary a little between seasons in the same area (Table 4.2b), tending to be smaller in late seasons than in early ones. In addition, clutches tend to be larger in some habitats than in others. For example, the swans in the Upper Thames area lay slightly larger clutches than those on the Lower Thames (Table 4.2c). In the Hebrides, those on the eutrophic lochs (the ones with better vegetation) lay larger clutches than those on the other freshwater lochs and on the brackish-water lochs (Table 4.2d).

Table 4.2(a): Clutch-size of Mute Swans in different areas

Oxford (Perrins and Reynolds 1967)	6.0
Oxford (Bacon 1980)	6.6
Oxford (Birkhead 1982)	6.9
Abbotsbury (Perrins and Ogilvie 1981)	4.8
Hebrides (Spray 1981)	6.1

Note: The difference between the earliest study in Oxford and the others may be due to a small sample collected in the city area, whereas the later ones covered many more 'rural' sites

Table 4.2(b): Clutch-size of Mute Swans in the Oxford area in different years

Year	1977	1978	1979	1980	1981
Clutch	6.4	6.9	6.15	7.74	7.03

Table 4.2(c): Clutch-size on the Upper and Lower Thames

Year	1980	1981	1982
Upper Thames	7.47	7.03	7.37
Lower Thames	7.07	7.03	7.36

Table 4.2(d): Clutch-size in different habitats in the Hebrides

Eutrophic lochs	Other freshwater lochs	Brackish-water lochs
6.31	4.75	5.49

Newly hatched cygnets do not usually stay at the nest for more than 48 hours

Hatching Success

The number of cygnets which hatch varies quite markedly. This is not, by and large, because of any inherent variation in the 'hatchability' of the eggs; only about one in ten of the eggs laid fails to hatch if they are incubated the full term (about 35 days). The variation arises mainly because a proportion of the nests fails to produce any cygnets at all (Table 4.3). The highest failure rates are observed in the Midlands study area, where about half of the nests fail.

The reasons for failure also differ from area to area. The commonest cause, both in the Oxford area and in the Midlands, however, was that the eggs were destroyed by people. The reasons for such destruction seem to vary. Usually it appears to be plain vandalism — the nest is full of broken eggs, bricks, bottles, etc. In one or two areas on small trout streams, it seems to be deliberate in that all the nests over quite a long stretch of river may be destroyed or the clutches markedly reduced. Not surprisingly, these effects vary locally. The Midlands swans, nesting in an area with a high human population, seem to suffer higher nesting losses than do the Oxford swans and, in both areas, losses are higher for nests near to, or in, the cities than for those in rural areas. In the most urban parts of the Midlands, the swans hatch less than half as many cygnets as do the birds which breed in the more rural areas around the cities.

Table 4.3: Percentage of nests lost before hatching

Oxford (Perrins and Reynolds 1967)	33%
Oxford (Bacon 1980)	29%
Oxford (Birkhead 1982)	30%
Midlands	49%
Hebrides	38%

The next most important cause of failure is flooding. Very heavy rain during laying or incubation may lead to extensive flooding and the loss of a number of nests. Again, there is local variation; nests along small streams seem to come off worst, possibly because these streams swell relatively more than the larger rivers, whose levels are mostly controlled by weirs. In the Oxford area, the nests on small streams are often only a little above the water level to start with, while those on the larger rivers are often higher above the water. Hence, nests on small streams may be more vulnerable to flooding.

Other losses are many and varied, although none of them individually seems to be important. A few clutches fail to hatch, possibly because they are infertile. A small number are deserted; usually, the reason for these desertions is not known, but at times excessive disturbance by humans seems the likely cause. Occasional nests fail because the female is taken by a fox, although one suspects that the combined defences of a pair of swans are normally sufficient to keep a fox at bay; exceptionally, the swans may even kill a fox, if it is in the water (Hunt 1815). There is one record of a clutch apparently being taken by badgers, which would be more difficult opponents to ward off.

When totting up the effects of these losses, it is worth keeping in mind that swans which lose their nest may lay a replacement clutch (two replacement clutches are occasionally laid if the birds lose two nests). Usually, only birds that lose their clutch fairly early in the season are inclined to replace it. Replacement clutches tend, however, to be smaller than the earlier ones and so are less productive. In addition, they tend to be less successful, perhaps because the pair is already breeding at a poor site. For example, in the Midlands, although about half the first clutches fail, about three-quarters of the replacement clutches do so; presumably, if the first clutch is lost to vandals and the birds re-nest in the same general area, they run a very high risk of being vandalised a second time. Such figures do not mean that there is little point in laying a replacement clutch; birds in good habitats which lose their first clutch from a natural cause, such as flooding, may have a good chance of producing young from a second attempt.

Survival Rates

Measuring the survival rates of swans takes a number of years, as a result of which there are rather few such studies. There are, however, some striking differences between the various populations which have been studied. In this section, we look at the survival rates at different stages in the life cycle and how they affect population size; detailed discussion of the causes of mortality is left to Chapter 7. We deal with the Abbotsbury population separately because of its unusual features.

Survival of Cygnets

The first detailed study of survival rates of cygnets was carried out in the Oxford area in the early part of the 1960s (Reynolds 1965). This showed that each pair of swans hatched, on average, about four young. This figure needs a little explanation. Over 90 per cent of the eggs that survive the full incubation period hatch; so that, in successful nests, the average brood-size at hatching is a little over five young (the average clutch being about six eggs). The figure of four young per pair takes into account those pairs which lose all their eggs. For example, imagine a population of 100 pairs in which each pair laid six eggs, and 20 of these pairs lost their clutch, while the remainder hatched five eggs each. The *individuals* with young would have an average brood of five, but the *population* as a whole would have only 400 young, an average of four per pair. Later, when we come to calculate the overall production, we need to use this information on a population basis.

The cygnets stay with their parents until at least September, a period of about 16-18 weeks. By this time, the young from the earliest nests are able to fly (we say that they have fledged), and the families start to break up as some young leave and join the non-breeding flocks. We calculated the survival rates during the family period and found that roughly half the young that hatched had died by September.

Thus, from an average clutch of six eggs, approximately four cygnets are produced, only two of which survive to fledging (again this figure includes unsuccessful pairs). Later studies in the Oxford area have suggested that this figure may have been a little on the low side. These early observations were based mainly on nests within the vicinity of Oxford, and rather few 'country' nests were included. By taking a larger study area, with more country nests, a rather higher success rate is obtained (Bacon 1980a). This is probably because country broods are in better habitats and less likely to be harassed by people, and because they provide better feeding; the result is that more cygnets survive from these broods.

The majority of the cygnets that die do so during the first few weeks after hatching. As the cygnets grow older, their chances of survival increase. For example, we followed the fate of 96 broods in the Upper Thames area. Of the 430 cygnets in these broods, 104 (24 per cent) died during the first ten weeks of life, while only five of the remaining 326 (1.5 per cent) died during the next ten weeks. Mortality is highest of all during the first week or two of life, and as many as 10-15 per cent of the cygnets may die within the first fortnight after hatching.

In the Midlands, the average brood-sizes at hatching and at fledging are smaller if pairs that fail completely are included; this is because more pairs lose their nests to vandalism. Apart from this, the results in the two areas are rather similar.

The situation in the Hebrides is somewhat different from that in central England. The Hebrides Mute Swans breed mainly on the lowland lochs, some of which are saline. The average brood-size in September is only about 1.8, lower than anywhere else. This is, however, an over-simplification, since there are marked differences in breeding success between the birds breeding on different types of lochs. The swans on the calcareous lochs on the 'machair' raised an average of 2.86 cygnets per pair, while those on the poorer lochs and the saline ones raised only about 1.5 cygnets per pair. Hence, those breeding on lochs on the machair were doing as well as — perhaps even slightly better than — those in England. There is, however, only a limited number of these good lochs, and about four-fifths of the birds bred on lochs of poorer quality.

Young cygnets often hitch a ride on the back of one of their parents

Survival of Immatures

Once the young swans have left their families they spend much of the next 18 months or so in the non-breeding flocks, and some spend con-siderably longer there than this. Although most of these birds tend to stay in the same general area, there is some movement between flocks and so survival is more difficult to measure than is the case with the broods or the breeding adults.

The most intensive study of the immatures was made at Oxford in the early 1960s, when there were large numbers of young birds in the non-breeding flocks. Because there were more of them, it was easier to obtain measurements on their survival than it has been at any time since then. Of the immature birds which were alive in September, approxi-mately two-thirds survived until the following June, a period of some nine months. Of those that survived until the age of one year, two-thirds survived to the age of two (a full year), and three-quarters survived from the age of two to three and from the age of three to four.

The comparable figures for the different studies are given in Table 4.4. In the Midlands, there is a rather lower survival of the young birds from their first September to the following June. Since the survival from hatching to September in the Midlands was a little better than in the Oxford area, however, the overall survival from hatching to the following June works out to be about the same (for Oxford, with a 50 per cent survival to September followed by a 67 per cent survival for the rest of their first year, the actual survival of the cygnets for the whole of their first year is .33 (.50 × .67 = .33); the comparable figures for the Midlands are .76 × .41 = .31). Thereafter, the survival of the immatures in the Midlands is very similar to that observed in Oxford.

Table 4.4: Annual survival of immature and adult Mute Swans in different areas

Age of birds	Oxford	Midlands	Hebrides	Abbotsbury
Fledging to 1 year (i.e. about 9 months)	67%	41%	58%	68%
One year to two	67%	68%	75%	90%
Two years to three	75%	69%	70%	90%
Three years to four	75%	77%	75%	90%
Over four years (= adult)	82%	85%	90%	94%

Note: Some of these figures are based on rather small series of years and some, particularly those for survival of first-year birds, are very variable between years (see text)

First-year survival in the Hebrides seems to be poorer than in the English studies. Not only do the birds lose more young prior to fledging, but only about 50 per cent of the young alive in October survive to the end of their first year.

From these figures we can see that the probability of survival of young birds improves steadily with time: the longer they live, the longer they are likely to live. There are probably two reasons for this. Firstly, small chicks are likely to be more vulnerable than larger ones; they can be taken by a wider range of predators, they are more easily chilled if not brooded, and they are less likely to survive on their own if they get separated from the rest of their family. Secondly, as they grow up they encounter — and presumably learn about — the hazards that face them. If they are lucky enough to avoid a particular hazard the first time, they may well be less likely to be caught out by it on later occasions. For example, many young swans injure or kill themselves by flying into objects such as boats, bridges and overhead wires; as they become more aware of their manoeuvring ability (or lack of it!), and perhaps better at manoeuvring, they may be less likely to fly into things.

Survival of Adults

In all the study areas, the survival of adults is higher than that of the immature birds. Again, this may be because adults are more experienced than immatures at avoiding hazards. In the case of breeding adults, however, it may also be because, once they have found a mate and a territory, they fly about less than the immature birds. There is no doubt that flying is a dangerous occupation for a swan, and this may be at the least a part of the explanation for the difference between the survival rates of immatures and adults.

In the Oxford area in the 1960s and early 1970s, about 82 per cent of the adults survived from one year to the next. In more recent years the figure has remained virtually the same, fluctuating between about 80 and 86 per cent. Similarly, the survival of adults in the Midlands has varied between about 79 per cent and 85 per cent.

The annual survival of the adults both at Abbotsbury and in the Hebrides is much higher than in central England. In the Hebrides the adult survival is about 90 per cent, and at Abbotsbury it has been as high as 94 per cent. In contrast, the adult swans on the Thames below Pangbourne have been known to have very poor survival rates, in one year as low as 68 per cent. These variations in the survival rate of adults have profound implications for the population, as we shall see in the next section.

Balance of Numbers

If a population of animals is to remain stable, the breeding members must produce sufficient young to replace those adults which die each year. Using the figures given above, we can see how many young swans survive to breeding age and compare this number with the number of adults which die each year. For simplicity we have assumed that the birds start breeding when four years old, though this varies quite a lot between individuals (page 86).

If we examine the survival rates of the Oxford birds in the 1960s, we can see how many young per pair survived to reach breeding age (Table 4.5). We can then ask 'Is this enough?' In this particular case, the annual survival rate of adults was 82 per cent (that is 18 per cent of the adults died each year), and this means that, on average, within each pair 0.36 adults die each year (0.18×2). Hence, if these figures were exactly right, the Oxford swan population needed 0.36 young birds to reach adulthood per pair each year. In actual fact about 0.43 did so, an excess over what was needed. This is as it should be for a healthy population; it needs to have a little surplus to make good the shortfalls which occur in particularly unfavourable years, such as when cygnet survival is very low or when a very severe winter leads to unusually high mortality.

Table 4.6 also shows these figures for Oxford in more recent years, alongside those for the Midlands and the Hebrides. The data for the immatures on the Thames and in the Hebrides are based on rather small numbers, so that the results need to be treated as rather provisional. This information suggests, however, that the Thames population is more or less holding its own, though this needs qualification. There are two main differences from the earlier data for the Oxford area. The productivity per pair is higher, probably because more rural nests are included than in the earlier study (page 70). Secondly, the figures mask some differences between the Oxford area and the Lower Thames. In the Oxford area, especially on the smaller rivers, the survival of adults is still around the 80 per cent mark, or even slightly better, and so the productivity is good enough to enable the swans to maintain their numbers in these areas. This is not, however, the case on the Lower Thames, where the annual adult mortality has been as high as 32 per cent with the result that the population in this area is not able to sustain itself without immigration. It is hardly surprising that the Mute Swan has declined so markedly there. We shall return to this problem later.

Although adult survival remains high in the Midlands, the population there has been declining steadily, since too few young survive to reach breeding age. Indeed, in this area the decline would presumably have been much faster had it not been for the fact that many of the young birds breed at three years of age instead of four.

Table 4.5: Productivity and survival in a population of Mute Swans

Each pair raises to September (50% survival of cygnets)	... 2.0 young
Each pair raises to 1 year old (67% survival for rest of year)	... 1.3 young
Each pair raises to 2 years old (67% survival in second year)	... 0.89 young
Each pair raises to 3 years old (75% survival in third year)	... 0.67 young
Each pair raises to 4 years old (75% survival in fourth year)	... 0.43 young

Note: Adult mortality was 18%, so 0.36 (2 × 0.18) young had to reach breeding age (four years) if the population was to maintain itself

Table 4.6: Productivity in different populations of Mute Swans

	Oxford	Midlands	Hebrides
No. hatching per pair	4.79	2.6	—
No. fledging per pair	2.13	1.92	1.77
No. surviving to age 1 per pair	1.43	.79	1.04
No. surviving to age 2 per pair	.96	.53	.78
No. surviving to age 3 per pair	.72	.37	.59
No. surviving to age 4 per pair	.54	.28	.44

The situation in the Hebrides is almost the opposite of that in the Midlands. Here, productivity is quite sufficient to replace the number of adults dying, since adult survival is high (Table 4.4). The increase has not, however, been as fast as one might have expected from the productivity of young birds, because the age at which they start to breed is later, probably at five years or older (page 67).

The Abbotsbury Population

The Abbotsbury population of Mute Swans is very different from the other British populations. The Mute Swans at Abbotsbury live in a very healthy environment, with large supplies of eel-grass. The food supply is so good that many other birds visit at different times of year. We have already mentioned that virtually all the swans there breed in a dense colony. The management of their young, once hatched, is unique, although perhaps similar management occurred elsewhere in the past. What happens is that the first seven pairs to hatch are put, together with their broods, in seven rearing pens. To these seven families are added other broods (but not the parents) as they hatch, until each 'family' may be made up of a pair with as many as 20 young. These broods are artificially fed until September, when they are nearly able to fly; they are then released. In the past, it was these birds which were kept and fattened for the table.

Those young which are not put in the pens are taken down to the water by their parents. Perhaps because there are large numbers of non-breeding swans, the survival of these cygnets is, however, very poor. This may be a feature of colonial swans in general rather than Abbotsbury in particular, since low survival of young cygnets has also been reported from the Danish swan colonies. For example, Danish colonial Mute Swans raise an average of only about 0.9 cygnets per pair, compared with 2.6 young for pairs which nest solitarily (Bloch 1970).

Hence, most of the young produced each year at Abbotsbury come from the pens, where cygnet survival is artificially high. It is not, therefore, possible to provide survival rates for cygnets from Abbotsbury for comparison with survival rates elsewhere.

Nevertheless, overall cygnet production (measured as cygnets produced per bird of breeding age) is both low and variable from year to year. There are a number of reasons for this. First, as many as one-fifth of the swans of breeding age (including birds that are known to have bred in previous years and whose mates are still present) fail to breed in certain years. Second, the number of pairs nesting successfully is variable; many can lose their nest if, as sometimes happens, a high spring tide comes through the colony. These two factors combined mean that often only a low proportion of birds of breeding age actually hatch young.

As mentioned, the large majority of the cygnets at Abbotsbury which survive until September are those which are raised in the pens; not surprisingly, these young birds have a very high survival rate during that period. After release, however, their survival is very variable; in poor winters with heavy winds, much of their main food may be uprooted

Plate 12. At Abbotsbury in Dorset, one adult pair of swans acts as foster parents for several broods of cygnets. They are all kept in pens until the cygnets are almost fully grown

and destroyed and the cygnets may not fare well. Survival from September to the following summer has been as low as 38 per cent. On the other hand, in good winters, the survival of these young is much higher than that recorded elsewhere. In 1979, 103 cygnets were released in September and of these no fewer than 95 (92 per cent) were still alive the following summer. Over eight years, the average survival rate of cygnets from September to the following summer was about 70 per cent, not very different from studies elsewhere, but very much more variable.

After the first year, survival is generally very good and is not even noticeably lower in the winters when the first-year birds survive poorly. The average survival of birds in their second and third years was 90 per cent. Again, this is very much higher than that recorded for immatures elsewhere. Indeed, it is not much lower than the survival rates of the adults, which have averaged almost 94 per cent, this also being higher than recorded anywhere else.

Several hundred Mute Swans can be seen at the Abbotsbury Swannery in Dorset

Age Structure of the Population

These large differences in survival rate between various populations mean that the age structures of these populations are very different. If we know the annual mortality of the birds, we can estimate the average expectation of further life of the adult swans by using the following formula:

$$\text{average expectation of further life} = \frac{(2 - m)}{(2 \times m)}$$

(m is the annual mortality)

In a population such as that on the Thames where the adult mortality is about 18 per cent, the average expectation of further life is only about five years, whereas one such as that in the Hebrides, with a 10 per cent mortality, has an average expectation of further life of about 9.5 years, and one with a mortality of about 6 per cent as at Abbotsbury has an average expectation of further life of 16 years!

Such large differences have two major effects on the different populations. Firstly, populations such as those at Abbotsbury and in the Hebrides have many more old, experienced adults among the breeders than is the case on the Thames. The longer the birds live, the less likely that both members of the pairs will die in the same year. This reduces the likelihood that traditional nest sites and feeding grounds will be forgotten; the older bird in each pair will have the local knowledge which may be important for successful breeding.

The second, and more important, aspect is that it needs many fewer young adults to enter the breeding population each year in order for the numbers of breeders to be maintained. In a population where the adult survival rate is 94 per cent, only 12 new breeders are needed each year to maintain a population of 100 breeding pairs, whereas, if the adults have only an 80 per cent survival rate, 40 new breeders would be needed each year to maintain a population of the same size.

The large variations in survival in these different populations show us that swans are able to maintain their numbers under a variety of different circumstances. This may seem surprising, but populations of wild animals have to have some considerable plasticity or they would not be able to survive. In populations with high adult survival rates, many of the young birds fail to establish themselves as breeders; they are unable to obtain a territory and have to eke out an existence in the flocks without one. In the late 1950s and early 1960s, those swans that failed to get a territory lived in the large flocks on the rivers. If the adult survival rate decreases, proportionately more of these young birds are able to obtain breeding territories and so the numbers of birds in the non-breeding flocks diminish. Both the Abbotsbury and the Hebridean Mute Swans are examples of populations in which there are many birds of breeding age that are not breeding. Although the details are not known, presumably many of these individuals cannot establish themselves as breeders because of the presence of large numbers of more dominant birds. This is fairly easy to understand in populations where the pairs are highly territorial; there is a limit to the numbers of pairs which can be fitted in. However, it is less clear why some birds of breeding age should be 'excluded' from breeding in a colony such as that at Abbotsbury, where it would seem possible to add more nests around the edge of the colony.

Age Structure of a Natural Population

We should perhaps ask two questions about the age structure of these populations: 'What was the natural situation in Britain?' and 'What is the lowest survival rate at which a swan population can maintain itself?'

The first of these is not easily answered. We can only guess that the situation in primaeval Britain was probably rather more like that in the Hebrides than that on the Thames. Although many of the pairs in the Hebrides live in areas with rather poor feeding, it seems likely that the adult Mute Swans would have had reasonably high survival rates and that, therefore, there would have been a low input of new, young adults into the breeding population each year. If this is the case, then the survival rates of adults on the Thames and in the Midlands are on the low side compared with natural populations.

Such a suggestion might well match with the fact that there would have been more natural predators in those times than there are today, when predators, apart from man, are more or less absent. In particular, there would have been more of the larger predators, such as bears and wolves, against which even birds as big as swans would have been unable to defend their nests; these animals are known to prey on Mute Swans in some areas (Sokolowski 1960). Bears were exterminated in southern England by about the tenth century, whereas wolves lived on in some parts of England until about 1500 and in the wilder parts of Scotland until about 1740. Once the young cygnets had hatched, however, the situation might have been very different, with the birds being relatively safe from predators, although White-tailed Eagles (*Haliaeetus albicilla*) seem to be able to kill swans.

The Limits for a Viable Population

From this stems the other question: What is the lowest survival rate with which a swan population can survive? We can make a guess. As we have seen, the 82 per cent survival rate of adult swans in the vicinity of Oxford at the beginning of the 1960s seems to have been sufficient to maintain their numbers; the fact that there were, at that time, large numbers of non-breeders in the flocks supports that view. Nevertheless, the survival rates of adults on the Lower Thames, which may be as low as 70 per cent, seem clearly too low; there is every reason to believe that this population is not able to maintain itself. We shall return to this point at a later stage.

There is, however, one difficulty about this last statement. We have seen that populations such as those at Abbotsbury and in the Hebrides can flourish with poor cygnet production and high adult survival. It is possible to speculate that the Lower Thames population could maintain itself with a low production of young if the adult survival was higher (the alternative, of low survival of adults coupled with good production of young, does not often occur in nature since, if the adults cannot flourish, the young are unlikely to be able to). The difficulty is that survival at all stages of the life cycle is poor, so that there is really no chance for them to maintain themselves at the moment. We think that this population is maintained only by immigration of young birds from surrounding areas.

It is important to stress that the presence of non-breeding flocks is crucial to the well-being of Mute Swan populations; they are the source of the new generations of breeders. This is especially true for those populations in which the adult survival rates are low and many new adults are needed each year. Since the swans need to be in these flocks for two or more years while they are maturing, there must be suitable places where the flocks can safely live and where the individuals in them will have a good chance of survival.

CHAPTER
5

Territories, Breeding and Life Cycle

In this chapter we follow the life cycle of a swan, from the moment a young cygnet leaves it parents, to finding a mate and eventually producing cygnets of its own. There are a number of points at which we could begin this story, but we choose to start at independence, the moment when cygnets leave the protection of their parents' territory and attempt to make it on their own.

Independence

The earliest-hatched young start to fly in September. From then on, the families start to break up. The actual time of the break-up varies greatly between broods. Some young stay with their parents until the following spring, and there are even exceptional records of young staying with their parents throughout the next breeding season. The break-up of the family may come about for a number of reasons, such as its taking flight because of some disturbance and then getting split up. In many cases, however, the parents play a major part in the break-up. Gradually, they become aggressive to their own young as well as to strangers on their territory. This leads eventually to the young being chased off the water on which they were raised, leaving the parents alone to start getting ready for the next breeding season. Many of the young that leave their parents' territory early in autumn, however, probably do so of their own accord.

Into the Flocks

Once the young birds have left, or been driven from, their natal site, they have to find a place to live. Normally, after a certain amount of wandering (though they seldom move very far), they find and join a flock of swans. These are composed mainly of immature birds aged between one and four (Minton 1971, Reynolds 1971). Nowadays, these non-breeding flocks occur commonly in towns, where the birds augment natural foods with bread supplied by the public. Occasionally, a flock of swans will try and settle on a breeding pair's territory, but a nesting pair will usually harass them persistently, even though they are not always capable of chasing them off (Scott 1984).

Finding a Mate

Immature swans congregate in flocks from the moment they leave their parents. While in these flocks, the juveniles start flirting with members of the opposite sex. Even first-year birds, still wearing their dark brown plumage, can be seen engaging in courtship behaviour. The young birds may not be physically capable of breeding, but it is probably valuable practice for later life. These non-breeding flocks are a vital part of the life cycle of the Mute Swan in that almost all the juveniles spend a high proportion of their 'teenage' years in them (Minton 1968).

The incidence of courtship among two-year-old swans in the flock is much higher than for first-year birds. This is not, however, too surprising, since some two-year-olds actually succeed in breeding, although most do not start until they are three to four years old. These interim courtships have been described as 'engagements' (Scott *et al.* 1972), but nobody knows how faithful pairs are at this time. It could be that most individuals are just 'playing the field' before they find the right mate.

The birds in these flocks have a clear pecking order in which some swans are dominant over others (Minton 1971, Lessells 1976). Older birds tend to be dominant over younger ones and males over females. The latter situation is probably due to males being larger than females. Once a female has paired, albeit temporarily, with a male, however, she rises up the dominance-hierarchy system to a position equal to that of her mate (Minton 1971).

Plate 13. A pair of immature Mute Swans goes through the courtship ritual

Establishing a Territory

Once a firm partnership has been established, which is normally in spring, the pair flies off to find a suitable breeding territory. Spring is one of the major periods when swans disperse, and it has been suggested that a peak in the recovery of dead swans at this time of year reflects an increase in the movement of swans looking for a suitable breeding territory (Figure 5.1). More often than not, the pair will return to the general area where the female was raised (Coleman and Minton 1979). Once there, however, it seems to be the male's job to try and establish the territory for them, though his mate may help defend the territory against other swans. Inexperienced Mute Swans do not usually breed in their first year on a territory, as they have to spend much more time in territorial disputes than do experienced pairs.

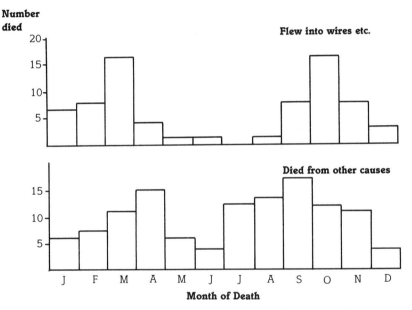

Figure 5.1: Monthly distribution of recorded deaths of Mute Swans in the Oxford study area. Deaths are divided into those birds which are known to have collided with an object in flight and all other causes (which were often not recorded by the finder of the bird). In both categories, there is a tendency for there to be more deaths in spring and autumn than in summer and midwinter. Deaths from oiling are not included

From Perrins and Reynolds (1967)

The possession of a territory is vital for all breeding activities, except pair formation. Such a territory may be a 2-km stretch of river, or merely an exclusive nest site as at Abbotsbury. Mature swans without an exclusive territory will not breed. Consequently, in years or areas where all the available territories are filled, some birds are prevented from breeding. In the early 1960s, there were a number of swans of four years and older in the large flocks on the River Thames, and the same is true today in the

Hebrides; these birds seem unable to find a breeding territory. This shortage of breeding territories is an important aspect of population ecology, as it can result in the regulation of numbers within a population (page 68).

In most parts of Britain, a suitable territory is an area of river a few kilometres long. There is a great deal of variability in the size of breeding territories, but on rivers around Oxford the average territory size was 2.5-3km (Bacon 1980a). On some of the best-quality rivers around Oxford the territories were smaller than this; but on the River Thames some pairs are over 15km apart, although formerly, when swans were abundant, they were much closer together.

Swans also establish breeding territories on lakes, ponds or gravel-pits, the latter having become increasingly common in the south of England over the last 40 years. Very few detailed studies have been carried out to determine the actual minimum territory size that a pair of breeding swans requires, but in Germany, on a shallow weedy lake, it was about 150 × 300m (Hilprecht 1970).

Colonially-breeding swans, such as those at Abbotsbury, will nest within a few metres of one another without serious disputes. This is the only place in Britain where swans nest like this. Several pairs, however, also nest in close proximity on nearby Radipole Lake in Weymouth, although the birds are usually in dense reeds out of sight of one another. Nobody seems to know why the swans in these areas should choose to nest in colonies, while those elsewhere seem to require much larger exclusive areas, but it must have something to do with a superabundance of food and/or a shortage of suitable nest sites along the rivers. Mute Swans also nest colonially in Poland and Denmark, where the nests can be as close together as 2m (Cramp and Simmons 1977).

Male Mute Swans have been known to fight to the death

Territorial Defence

Once they have established a territory, swans defend it to prevent intruders from trying to set up their own territory nearby. The most rigorous defence takes place early in the year, just prior to and during the breeding season, that is from late February through to April or May. At first the male and female move around together, regularly visiting the limits of their territory. Whenever they encounter other swans, they will try to chase them off. Intruding youngsters are usually no problem and are easily persuaded to leave by a charging adult male. Established adult pairs on the edge of their territory, however, present a very different problem; a long battle may ensue before both pairs retire behind their common boundary.

Both sexes may perform antagonistic behaviour, but it is more common and exaggerated in males. The main threat display involves the raising of the secondary feathers — the middle section of the wings — which partly cover the swan's back. At the same time, the feathers on the neck are fluffed up and the neck is arched over the back. The swan then swims in a very exaggerated, jerky manner, performing his so-called 'busking' display. The jerkiness comes about because the bird paddles with both feet simultaneously, instead of alternately as he usually does. Two territorial males may parade along their boundary until both decide that they have reached an honourable draw or, alternatively, one charges the other. In the latter case, the attacker will fly at the other bird, beating his wings and feet on the water. If this impresses the other bird sufficiently, it will give way and try to escape. Not all territorial disputes, however, are resolved so easily and fights may occur.

Occasionally a serious fight will follow, where necks become entwined and the rivals beat each other with their wings. The fight is accompanied by snorting and the winner usually ends up mounting his opponent, pecking and beating him. Very rarely, fights like this can result in deaths. We know of two instances in the Oxford area in which one male killed another in a territorial dispute. In both cases, an experienced male killed a young bird which was trying to set up a territory in part of an already established territory. In the first, one young pair tried to nest so close to the older pair that we were amazed that both pairs actually got as far as laying eggs, but then at that stage the trouble began. The young pair nested on a pond, within sight of the older pair on a nearby river not more than 150 m away. We do not know all the details in this case, but the result was a fight in which the young male was killed. In the other case, the young pair nested in what might have seemed to them to be a vacant territory; what they did not realise was that the site was a favourite spot for two older pairs to bring their newly hatched families. For most of the year, these older pairs maintained exclusive territories and kept apart from each other. The young pair was very unlucky and, because they laid their eggs later than the older pairs, the female was still incubating when both older families appeared on the stream. Consequently, the young male had to try to defend his territory against two older males, when even one would have been a real trial. Eventually, he was beaten to death by one of the older males in a local farmer's garden, the farmer witnessing the fight.

Serious fights, however, are normally rare and the weaker bird usually escapes with few injuries. The loser indicates submission by sleeking both its body and wing feathers in what looks like an attempt to appear as inconspicuous as possible and in this way tries to reduce his adversary's aggression in order to make good his escape.

Plate 14. A large cob signals his intent by fluffing his feathers, raising his wings and 'busking' towards his opponent

Marriage and Divorce

One of the most common questions we are asked is 'Do swans really mate for life?' Well, the answer is that, just like human beings, some do and some don't! It is true to say that the majority of pairs remain together as long as their partner is alive. Occasionally, birds will change their partner even while their mate is still alive, but divorce is very rare: less than 3 per cent per annum among established breeding pairs which breed successfully, and only slightly more frequent, around 9 per cent, among pairs which have attempted to breed and failed (Table 5.1) (Minton 1968).

Table 5.1: The marital status of paired Mute Swans in subsequent years

	No. of pairs alive	No. of individuals dead or missing	Status in following year			
			Same mate No.	Same mate %	New mate %	Not paired %
Breeding						
1961	100	22	84	84	5	11
1962	86	41	46	54	24	22
1963	79	28	68	86	6	8
1964	113	28	98	87	7	6
1965	129	24	108	84	12	4
1966	101	35	88	87	11	2
Non-breeding						
1961	17	16	14	82	6	12
1962	31	17	10	34	33	33
1963	39	17	18	46	37	17
1964	33	16	26	79	6	15
1965	29	25	12	41	31	28
1966	22	23	12	55	32	13

From Minton (1968)

Successful older swans will almost certainly have several mates in their lifetime. Clive Minton (1968), in his detailed study on this subject, recorded some old swans which had had as many as four mates during their lives. Clearly, these findings dispel the romantic myth that a bereaved swan will never take another mate.

It appears that if a female loses her mate she usually returns to the flock to find another, unless by chance she finds a suitable lone male. Breeding males, once widowed, however, frequently remain on, and defend, their territory even without a female and are less likely to find another partner and re-mate. Minton cites an example of a male swan which remained and defended its territory, built a nest by itself, and even 'incubated' imaginary eggs in the empty nest for several weeks. Such differences in behaviour between the sexes may be partially explained by the fact that a lone female would have more difficulty in defending a territory than would a solitary male.

As mentioned earlier, divorce among swans is fairly rare. Change of partners is usually the result of death or disappearance of the old mate. As with humans, however, there are numerous reasons and permutations for swan divorces. Some of the details make fascinating reading. Wife-swapping is not unknown and usually occurs between pairs in adjacent territories. Such exchanges often happen after a furious boundary dispute, and one cannot be sure whether the new partnerships were planned or accidental!

Some marriages obviously work well. We had one pair which bred together for 19 consecutive seasons. In terms of reproductive success, such fidelity is advantageous, as the pair had great cumulative experience. In general, older and more experienced birds are more successful in producing young, as is explained later in this chapter.

Odd Couples

There are numerous other examples of 'odd pairings', for instance, the relationships between closely-related individuals. Although there have been several records of fathers pairing with daughters, there have been very few examples of incestuous pairs successfully rearing cygnets. Clive Minton, in his detailed study (1968), mentions only close associations, not successful matings.

Homosexual pairings have been recorded, more often than not in captivity (Heinroth 1911). Such associations have also been known to occur at the Abbotsbury Swannery (Low 1935): two males got together and even went so far as building a nest. Female associations, too, have been recorded and these can even lead to the production of eggs, although they are of course infertile (Scott *et al.* 1972). Most of these sexual aberrations occur in zoos or collections where there is an unbalanced sex ratio. There is very little evidence to suggest that they are at all frequent in the wild.

Extra-marital Affairs

Monogamy is the rule in swans, but polygamy occurs very occasionally. The limited number of records which refer to polygamy usually occur when a pair already has eggs and the female is incubating (Hilprecht 1970, Scott *et al.* 1972). During this long process, the male has plenty of time, if he gets the opportunity, to seek extra copulations. In normal circumstances any sexually receptive female will be closely guarded by her mate, but if the pair's territory is adjacent to, or overlaps, the range of a number of flock birds, as is often the case at Henley-on-Thames, other males may sneak in to the territory and mate with the female. In one case, an unattached female copulated with an already mated male, building a nest only 10 m away from the first nest and successfully hatching a brood of cygnets (Portielje 1936).

Winter Territoriality

Unlike migratory swans, many British Mute Swans maintain their territories throughout the year, and will leave only if the weather is so severe that the water freezes over. There is, however, considerable variation in this behaviour. In more northerly latitudes, such as in Sweden, Mute Swan pairs normally leave their territory in winter to join the flock birds (Andersen-Harild 1978). In a detailed study of winter territoriality, Dafila Scott (1984) found that the variation in behaviour was associated with temperature and the amount of food in the territory. In general, pairs left their territory only during the coldest months, and pairs on the territories with the best food supplies stayed and defended them the longest. It would seem that the best strategy for all pairs would be to stay on their territory as long as the food supply lasts. If this is for the whole year, so much the better, since this decreases the chances of their losing their territory to another pair.

In winter, the territories of swans are sometimes less exclusive than in the breeding season. Occasionally, pairs share their home with a large flock of immature swans. During the first few days after the flock has arrived, the indignant territorial cob, whose privacy has been disturbed, will spend a great deal of time and energy in chasing the younger birds. Occasionally, such aggressive actions will pay off and the younger birds will give up and try their luck elsewhere. But, if suitable feeding places for the immature swans are limited and if they are not deterred by the adult pair, the flock will succeed in staying and the older birds become resigned to their presence. In these cases, the size of the flock can sometimes be important. In a large flock, any one individual is likely to be chased less and, as a result, the territorial birds would have to do more work to deter the whole flock.

Nest Site

The location of the nest site must depend in part on there being enough vegetation nearby. At the swan colony in Abbotsbury, Dorset, where 50 or more pairs may nest, the warden provides most of the nest material for the swans. Experienced swans normally select a site which will withstand all but the worst floods. In some very wet springs, however, all the nests on certain stretches of river will be lost, no matter where the swans nest. The choice of nest site does not always seem particularly sensible. Around Oxford one pair regularly bred on a canal towpath, but the swans' fearsome reputation meant that most people respected them and left them alone, with the result that they successfully hatched all of their eggs. Their success should also be credited to local vigilantes — not uncommon where swans nest in built-up areas — who guarded the swans throughout the incubation period.

In addition to normally choosing a secluded site, swans also select sites on a bank with easy access to and from the water. They need to be able to walk, rather than fly, to and from the nest: as they are doubtless safer on water than on land, they need the chance of easy and rapid access to the water. In certain areas, the wash from boats has led to the banks becoming undercut and steep and, because of the importance of easy access to nest sites, swans have found it progressively harder to find suitable sites on the large rivers. On the lower stretches of the Thames, many pairs actually nest off the river, up little side-streams, probably partly for this reason.

Plate 15. Mute Swans usually require an exclusive breeding territory of a few kilometres of river. Here at Abbotsbury in Dorset, however, about 50 pairs of swans nest in fairly close proximity to one another

Nests tend to be in the same site year after year, and there are two reasons why this occurs. Firstly, swans are fairly long-lived so that in many cases at least one of the pair is likely to survive from one year to the next and re-select the same nest site. In other cases, where both birds of a pair are new, they may still build on the same site as the previous pair; often the number of suitable sites is very restricted, so it is hardly surprising that two pairs of swans find the same small patch of land attractive, especially if it is the only island in a lake or gravel-pit.

Nest-building

Once a pair has established a breeding territory, the two can get on with the business of building a nest, mating and producing a family. Mute Swans normally nest very close to the water, either alongside a river or lake or occasionally, in certain areas such as some places in Denmark, by the sea. Sometimes they make nests on solid ground and sometimes they build large mounds of vegetation in shallow water.

At least on some occasions, the male chooses a site and starts to build there. The female may or may not accept her mate's choice of site, with the result that the male may start several nests before his mate approves of one (MacSwiney 1971). Once the birds have agreed on a site, both sexes help to build the nest. This is made of vegetation such as rushes and reeds; the swans use only material from the close proximity of the nest. As a result, the actual material used depends totally on the nest site; in a reedbed the nest will be built of reeds, while on rocky shores in Scotland and the Baltic it may be built entirely of seaweed. The male normally passes the vegetation to the female, who sits on the nest and shapes it. Nests vary enormously in size; in some cases they can be 3m in diameter, while in others, if there is not much vegetation close at hand, they may contain only a little material. A large swan's nest can take up to ten days to complete, is normally substantial enough to withstand a certain amount of flooding, and may even form the foundation for the following year's nest. On top of the nest there is usually a shallow depression of a few centimetres where the female may, sometimes, add a little down (though never anything like as much as in a duck's nest) to form the 'cup' in which the eggs are laid.

Both sexes help to build the substantial nest

Mating

In the early days of courtship, sexual activity is limited to mutual head-turning. This attractive display involves both birds facing each other, fluffing their neck feathers, giving a few snorts and then indulging in a period of head-turning. Sometimes the display lasts only a few seconds, but in the build-up to mating it can last quite a lot longer (Huxley 1947, Boase 1959, Johnsgard 1965). Mating and courtship displays take place mostly prior to egg-laying, but they are not exclusive to this time of year and occur far more frequently than is required to fertilise the clutch (Boase 1959). They may be an important factor in maintaining the pair bond.

A pair of mating swans

Once this preliminary activity is completed, an elaborate pre-copulatory display then takes place. The first component involves both swans alternately dipping their heads beneath the water. This goes on for a few minutes until the birds' actions become synchronised. With the two still facing each other, with their necks entwined, the male then pushes onto the female's back as she turns around. When the male has mounted the female, he then holds her neck in his beak. The first time anyone observes this sequence he or she will probably think that one bird is trying to drown another, rather than mate with it! The female's head often disappears for several seconds at a time, and it is with some relief that you finally see the male pull his partner's head above water again. After copulation, both birds make a number of snorting-like calls, turn to face each other, and then rise out of the water paddling their feet. Both birds will then go through a vigorous washing and preening session.

Egg-laying and Clutch-size

The eggs are usually laid in late March, April or the first half of May. We have, however, recorded egg-laying as early as 7 March and as late as early June. In 1959, R.J. Hill wrote to HM Swan Keeper that he 'even saw some [cygnets] hatching out in September'; the eggs in this clutch were presumably not laid until about mid-July, an exceptionally late date.

The female usually lays her eggs on alternate days, and more often than not in the morning. Laying does not normally commence until the nest is built, but occasionally a female will lay her eggs before this: it is a strange sight to come across a solitary swan's egg deposited on a river-bank with no nest to be seen. As the egg-laying interval is around two days, a large clutch of ten or eleven eggs can take three weeks to complete. In the egg-laying period, before the clutch is complete, the male will often sit on the eggs and guard them while the female continues to feed.

Clutch-size in the Mute Swan declines, almost linearly, as the season progresses (Figure 5.2). Irrespective of location, it is the early layers which produce the large clutches, but there is a degree of variation in the average clutch-size both between and within areas (page 70). The average clutch-size for the Mute Swan in Britain is around six eggs, with a range from about three to 12. Swans have only one brood a year but, occasionally, a repeat clutch may be laid if for some reason the first clutch is destroyed. Repeat clutches tend to contain fewer, smaller eggs (Bacon 1980a).

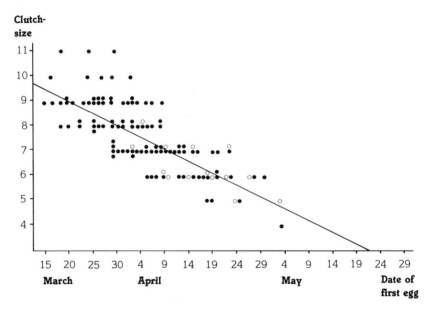

Figure 5.2: This figure shows the usual relationship between clutch-size and the date the first egg is laid. Open circles denote repeat clutches.

From Reynolds (1972)

We do not know what actually triggers egg-laying in swans. In most bird species, the individuals become more sexually active as the days lengthen in spring. The actual date on which Mute Swans start laying, however, varies in relation to a number of factors. One of these is winter temperature: the warmer the months of December, January and February, the earlier the swans start laying (Figure 5.3). This link with winter temperature almost certainly arises because temperature affects plant growth (the food supply), which in turn affects clutch-size and breeding success.

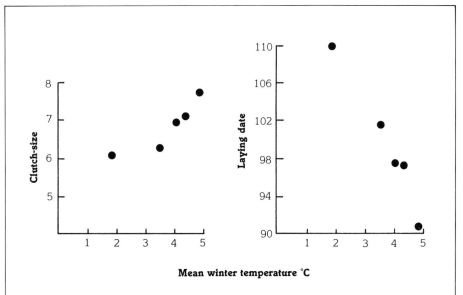

Mean winter temperature °C

Figure 5.3: The relationship between mean winter temperature (the months of December, January and February) and laying date and clutch-size. Each point represents the mean for one of the years through 1977-81

From Birkhead *et al.* (1983)

The factors affecting clutch-size are important because they determine the number of young produced. There are, however, a lot of factors which play significant roles in the eventual breeding success of a pair of Mute Swans. For example, the length of time a pair of swans has been together is important. An experienced breeding pair (which has bred together at least once) will lay earlier, produce a larger clutch and produce more cygnets than an inexperienced pair (which has not bred before) (Table 5.2). This is not too surprising, as more experienced birds should know the best feeding sites within a territory, and will almost certainly have to spend less time defending that territory against intruders.

Table 5.2: Laying date, clutch-size and number of cygnets fledged for experienced and inexperienced pairs of Mute Swans from the Oxford study area in 1978

	Mean laying date (days from 1 Jan)	**Mean clutch-size**	**Mean number of cygnets fledged**
Experienced	96	7.0	2.8
Inexperienced	108	5.7	1.7

From Birkhead *et al.* (1983)

The Eggs

The average swan egg weighs around 350g and measures 12 × 7cm. The shell is about 1mm thick, and is composed mostly of calcium. Inside the egg is, as everyone knows, the white and the yolk. The yolk contains a lot of fat and protein for the developing embryo, while the white is made up of protein and water. In the Mute Swan, it appears that larger eggs contain relatively more yolk and more fats in the yolk (Birkhead 1984). This means that larger eggs may produce hatchlings with proportionately larger yolk reserves. The cygnets which hatch from such eggs may have a better chance of surviving than those from eggs with smaller reserves. Eggs vary enormously in their composition — that is the quantity of the various constituents such as calcium, water and protein — from one female to the next, but in general those laid by any particular female tend to be fairly constant in size and composition.

Unincubated swans' eggs appear to be remarkably durable. One pair of swans near Oxford laid two eggs. The nest then got flooded by a rapidly rising river and the eggs remained underwater for a couple of days. After the flood had subsided, the female laid nine more eggs and all 11 eggs hatched successfully.

Incubation

Only when the clutch is complete does the female start the long process of incubation. Unlike the male, she has a brood patch — a bare patch of skin on her breast, richly supplied with blood vessels, to keep the eggs warm. Incubation normally lasts 35 days and during that time the female feeds very little, if at all. Although the male may sit on the eggs from time to time, he does not do any real incubation. Towards the end of incubation the female may get very weak through lack of food, and can often be picked off the nest, weighing just two-thirds of her normal weight. It has been known for a female to sit for over 50 days on an infertile or dead clutch of eggs (Boase 1959).

Swans are large enough to deter most predators

Predation of Eggs

We have never known any predator other than humans take a swan's egg. Human predation, however, is very common, either from 'mantelpiece' collectors or from 'I dare you' types. Usually, swans can frighten off most would-be predators by using their wings and beaks, and it is the cob that does most of the nest defence. The response of the female will depend on how far she is into incubation; in the early stages when she is still strong she can be quite aggressive, but later on she tends just to sit tight.

Cygnets

The young emerge from the eggs some 48 hours after they make the first cracks in the shell. Usually, all the eggs hatch within about 24 hours of each other, and the cygnets remain in the nest for 24-48 hours before taking to the water. Not uncommonly, the pen may remain on the nest, brooding late-hatched young or unhatched eggs, while the cob looks after the cygnets that are on the water. This situation generally lasts only a short time, since the pen soon deserts the nest after the last young has left, but occasionally she may be unwilling to leave unhatched eggs and this may lead to problems.

Young cygnets are normally light grey in colour with white underparts. Some young, however, are born with white down similar in colour to their parents, the so-called 'Polish' cygnets (see page 8).

Even the first downy plumage of the cygnets is remarkably waterproof. The cygnets maintain this waterproofing — as they will for the rest of their lives — by constant preening and by rubbing of preen oil onto their feathers. This oil comes from the preen gland, which is situated on the rump, just forward of the base of the tail. The birds transfer the oil by picking it up on the bill and distributing it on the feathers. They cannot, of course, reach the feathers on top of their head with their bill, hence the rather odd antics one can see of birds rubbing their head on the base of the tail as they try to rub preen oil onto the head feathers.

The newly hatched cygnet weighs about 220 g, roughly two-thirds of the weight of the fresh egg. Of the lost third, roughly one-third is eggshell and the remaining two-thirds are used up during development or consist of water lost by evaporation from the egg. The 'weight' of the young cygnet includes some 25 per cent of the yolk from the egg that it had not metabolised by the time it hatched (Heinroth and Heinroth 1928). This is important for the cygnet, because it can live on this food store for some days. In a brood of cygnets which had some deformity that prevented them from feeding, the young birds survived for ten days on this stored yolk (Kear 1965). Clearly, this is an important reserve during the first few days of life when the young birds are learning to fend for themselves. In spite of the waterproofing, they still need to be kept warm in cold weather and so it is important for them to stay with their mother and be brooded when necessary.

Although it may seem wise for the swans to choose a nest site where the cygnets have ready access to good feeding, this does not appear to be one of their priorities, since parents are quite prepared to take the newly hatched cygnets some distance to suitable feeding areas. There are a number of records of swans nesting on small ponds and, when the young hatch, leading them on hazardous cross-country journeys, which may involve crossing a railway line or busy road, to another site. Some such journeys result in the parents losing all or most of their chicks, and yet they may nest in the same site in successive years. One pair that was more successful than this nested for several years on a very shallow lake just behind the beach near Bexington, about 4 km west of Abbotsbury in Dorset. This lake was quite unsuitable for raising cygnets, since it often dried up in the summer. As soon as the young hatched, the parents led them across the beach and into the sea, swimming with them eastwards to make landfall on the Chesil Bank, which they crossed and then stayed on the Fleet. Stevenson (1890) records an old female who regularly used to spend the winter on the Yare in Norfolk, between Thorpe and Whitlingham, but who always nested on Surlingham Broad. As soon as the young had hatched, she took them on her back and swam back to her wintering area, a distance of some 10 km or so. These movements are interesting in that the birds must know where they are going and, although they would normally never move between the two areas 'on foot', they must know how to get there either by swimming or by walking when they have small young (page 114).

Both adults stay with the cygnets throughout the summer. When the young are small, they may ride on their parents' backs for some of the time. This is probably a valuable aid to survival, since such young birds are prone to predation from various enemies. Many chicks disappear when they are very young, and we suspect that pike are responsible. Since a young cygnet weighs only about 220 g, it is easily swallowed by pike of even moderate size. When on the move with larger young, the pen characteristically leads the young to the next feeding site while the cob provides the rearguard.

Although the young cygnets can feed themselves from the early stages, they may need help with reaching the food. If they are living on waters with little emergent vegetation, their parents pull up vegetation which is out of reach of the cygnets' short necks. Swans with young cygnets may also paddle vigorously with their feet, an action which apparently stirs up food items on the bottom and brings them within reach of the small cygnets. As the cygnets grow larger, they become entirely dependent on their own efforts to get food.

Apart from leading them to good feeding and guarding them, the parents do not provide food nor do they try to help any weaklings. Indeed, the reverse is often the case. It frequently happens that, if a chick becomes sickly or falls behind the others in its growth, the parents persistently attack it and try to chase it away; eventually these cygnets normally perish. Such swans get the reputation of being poor parents or 'cruel'. It seems at least possible that the opposite is the case. If a chick is not doing well, it probably has only a poor chance of growing up to become an adult, so there is little point in the parents taking good care of it. Indeed, since the chick may be failing because it is diseased or carries a heavy load of parasites, it may well be better for the health of the family that it is driven away. It may seem cruel, but such behaviour could have developed through natural selection, since the rest of the brood may stand a better chance in the absence of a sickly chick than in its presence.

The 120-150 days that a Mute Swan takes to reach the flying stage is considerably longer than for some of the other swans. Bewick's Swans can fly at about 40-45 days and Whoopers at 70 days. These birds, particularly the Bewick's which breed in the high Arctic, have a race against time to get their young to the flying stage before the area freezes over in the autumn. Compared with the Mute Swan, cygnets of the other species eat a considerable number of insects, which are richer in proteins than the vegetable diet of Mute Swan young. In addition, the northern swans are raised in an area where there is 24 hours of daylight, which means that they can feed more or less the whole time. The latter fact is likely to be an important part of the explanation for their shorter fledging period, since Bewick's Swans raised in captivity in England grow more slowly (Scott *et al.* 1972).

Moult

Swans have a very large number of feathers (page 6). These provide important waterproofing, insulation and streamlining, to say nothing of the striking white coloration. Feathers do not last forever, though, and like most birds swans replace their feathers once a year. A great many feathers are replaced in a moult after the breeding season, in July and August. The moult is a time of considerable energy demand.

As with most wildfowl, swans are flightless during their annual moult, which takes about 4-7 weeks, the period apparently varying between different areas. Breeding swans moult while their young are still unable to fly. This is clearly advantageous since it means that, by the time the young are on the wing, the parents can also fly again so that, if necessary, the whole family can fly to another site. The two parents moult their flight feathers at different times, the pen usually starting her moult soon after the young have hatched and the cob not until later when his mate's flight feathers are well grown. Since swans rely to a considerable extent on the use of their wings in fights and in the defence of their brood against enemies, it is probably beneficial for pairs to stagger their moult in this way so that one parent is always capable of defending its family without damaging its growing quills. In non-breeding flocks, birds of both sexes shed their flight feathers at the same time. In the arctic-breeding Bewick's Swans, both sexes moult at the same time as there is no opportunity at that latitude for a staggered moult.

The act of replacing all these feathers is expensive in the energetic sense in that the birds need considerable amounts of extra food in order to form the new feathers (page 112). Moulting birds may rely on stored reserves and may lose up to 1 kg of weight during the moulting period. They are also presumably less waterproof and less well insulated, since they are missing a lot of their feathers. This is probably one of the reasons why they moult in late summer: it is the warmest time of year and the time when food is still plentiful.

Because they are flightless, and therefore vulnerable, at this time, many non-breeding moulting birds may move to safe areas, often on large bodies of water such as lakes or estuaries, to moult. They return to their normal areas once they can fly again.

Occasionally, one sees a swan with very ragged, old flight feathers. These birds seem to have been injured in some way and have been unable to replace their feathers. If enough of the feathers are damaged, the bird will not be able to fly. Pinioning is achieved by the same principle: if a small section of the outer wing is removed when the bird is small, such that its primaries cannot grow, the bird will never be able to fly. The same effect can be achieved temporarily by cutting off some of the larger feathers; once these are shed at the next moult, the bird will be able to fly normally again.

CHAPTER

6

Food and Feeding

The Mute Swan, like other swans, is totally herbivorous. Only one other group of birds, the geese, have such a restricted vegetarian diet and these, of course, are close relatives of the swans. Almost all other birds which mainly eat plants also take in some animal food; for example, young game birds, when growing rapidly, eat many insects. The basic problem with herbivory is that plant material contains a lot of cellulose, which birds cannot break down easily. Vegetarian mammals have stomachs that contain bacteria capable of breaking down cellulose, but in order to do this efficiently the animal must retain its food for some time. This means that they need a large, heavy stomach. This is not practical for a bird, since it could not fly if weighed down by such an organ. So, birds with a vegetarian diet require a number of special-isations.

The first problem in the case of a bird like the swan is how to pull up grass or other vegetation, for, unlike mammals such as cows and sheep, it has no teeth to cut the vegetation. Swans have quite strong jaw muscles which enable them to grab a tight hold of grass or aquatic vege-tation that they intend to consume. In addition, the bill and tongue have horny serrations along their length, enabling the birds to grip the food tightly. The upper and lower sections of the bill work like a pair of forceps, and the food is torn rather than cut.

The next problem is that the swan has no teeth to grind the food down and as a result the food, once it has been swallowed, passes down the gullet (oesophagus) intact. A swan, like many other birds, has its own version of a set of teeth in its gizzard (stomach). An adult swan has a gizzard roughly the size of a tennis ball which is made up of two separate blocks of muscle arranged opposite each other. Although the gizzard is very strong, it is not itself capable of breaking down the plant cell walls — essential if the swan is to absorb the plant's nutrients. Like the domestic hen, the swan collects grit and mixes it up with its food; by the muscular action of the gizzard, grinding the food and the grit together, the plant cells are broken down. The gizzard itself, which acts rather like a coffee grinder, has a special protective coat to prevent it from grinding itself to pieces. The grit, usually ingested in the form of gravel, is quickly worn down and needs to be replaced often. So far as we know, no-one has actually estimated how much gravel a healthy swan ingests in a day. Swans can, however, frequently be seen 'eating' mouthfuls of gravel. The swan's digestive system is dependent on the bird being able to find sufficient grit for efficient digestion. This is an important part of the swan's ecology since the bird, in its search for small hard objects to use as grit, at times encounters anglers' lead weights which it swallows just like grit, and this leads to problems (see Chapter 7).

The Mute Swan has a fairly inefficient digestive system and, without the commensal bacteria possessed by certain (mammalian) vegetarians, it has only a limited ability to digest vegetable matter. To compensate partly for this, the swan has a very large intake of food, out of which it takes relatively little nutrient. As a result, birds such as swans and geese have to spend a large proportion of their day feeding.

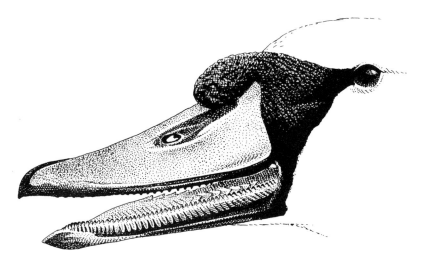

The horny serrations on the swan's bill and tongue enable it to grasp a tight hold of vegetation

Feeding Methods

Swans use a number of methods to obtain food, and in particular they use their long necks to reach food that would otherwise be unobtainable. It is not often realised that swans also reach upward for food, rather like a grazing giraffe. We have frequently watched them stretch up

Plate 16. 'Bottoms-up!' Up-ending swans can reach food some 90 cm beneath the water surface

for leaves of crack willow *Salix fragilis*, although what makes these so attractive we do not know. The long neck is made up of 25 bones — more than in other birds, and 18 more than in a giraffe's neck — and it often comes in useful for reaching food not available to other species. The long neck, however, is best known in relation to another feeding technique, known as 'up-ending'. By sticking their bottoms and feet in the air, swans can reach some 90cm below the water surface. In shallow water, this enables them to reach a wide range of tubers and plant roots; in deeper water, they may be able to reach only the tops of plants, but they can still break off pieces and pull them up. This ungainly position can be maintained for as long as 30 seconds, but usually they stay up-ended for only about 15 seconds (Scott *et al.* 1972).

When feeding in shallow water, the swans can use alternative feeding methods and this is where they either 'dip' or 'dabble'. Dipping also involves submerging the head and neck, but, instead of stretching to the limit, the swan arches its neck into an 'S' shape and lays its chin flat along the river or lake bed. Such a feeding method is confined to water of about 30cm in depth, and the swan keeps its head submerged for only about ten seconds. During submergence, just as when up-ending, swans can swallow the ingested food without having to surface to breathe. Swans, like ducks, will also dabble; they place their bill horizontally along the water, draw the water through a partially open bill, close it and then squirt the water out along the sides of the bill, through the bill lamellae. The horny serrations help the bill to filter out small food items such as algae and duckweed.

Aquatic feeding is often accompanied by vigorous 'running-on-the-spot' or 'foot-paddling'. The swan raises itself partially out of the water and creates water currents by alternately paddling its feet. This activity, which accompanies up-ending and dipping, helps stir up any food that may be lying on the bottom and also exposes various roots and rhizomes by washing the mud away. The food is then pulled to the surface, ripped apart and eaten. Mute Swans can create quite large holes in shallow water by foot-paddling.

Swans do not always feed on or in water. They will often eat grass and other types of terrestrial vegetation. Most grazing occurs in the late winter and spring, when pondweeds such as *Potamogeton* and *Elodea* have died down. The timing of this switch has not been studied in detail, but it seems to vary from place to place. Subjectively, however, what seems to happen is that breeding pairs remain on their territory and feed on aquatic food plants such as water-crowfoot *Ranunculus* and pondweed until late autumn; when this type of food becomes scarce, the cygnets are driven off their parents' territory, and the breeding pair then returns to feeding on the grass, or on whatever grows in the nearby fields.

Many of the flocks live off the 'country' in spring, summer and early winter, but spend an increasing amount of time in late winter in towns, where they depend on the public to a large extent for food. Numerous gravel-pits and other lakes can be relied on to provide a good supply of *Elodea*, which seems to last longer into winter than other aquatic vegetation. Large flocks of up to 100 birds can often be seen on well-stocked gravel-pits well into the winter. Needless to say, once a flock becomes established, with many birds feeding in a relatively confined space, the food does not last long, especially since at this time of year it is not growing rapidly. Once the food is used up or has died down, these flocks will turn their attentions to grasslands and come into towns. In very late winter, some also turn to winter cereals (see later in this chapter).

An 'up-ended' swan grazing on the river floor

Swans are almost exclusively diurnal — daytime — feeders. In winter, when undisturbed, Mute Swans' feeding activities increase during the day, reaching a peak some three hours after sunrise and continuing until a little after dark (Owen and Cadbury 1975).

Food

There have been several studies on the food of the Mute Swan and in this section we present a brief summary of their findings. Unfortunately, most of these studies were fairly restricted in that they took place during the summer only, and several were restricted to salt or brackish water.

In general, swans feed mainly on the leaves and stems of submerged aquatic plants such as crowfoot *Ranunculus* and pondweed *Potamogeton*. In marshland areas, the roots, tubers and stolons of aquatic saltmarsh succulents such as *Plantago* and *Aster* are favoured. Emergent vegetation is not often taken, but the stems and leaves of a few species are sometimes eaten. As mentioned earlier, willow leaves seem popular; swans will even eat them in large quantities in autumn, after they have fallen. It is not uncommon to see a swan 'moored' in mid-stream, picking up the willow leaves as they float past. Seeds are not actively sought, but in recent years Mute Swans have taken to gleaning both cereals and dumped grain, and they will regularly feed on agricultural pasture.

In Britain, there have been only a couple of detailed field studies on the food of the Mute Swan. The first, which was carried out by Gillham (1956), we deal with in this section and the second, by Scott (Scott and Birkhead 1983), we look at later in this chapter in the section on food demands.

Gillham's study was on a flock of about 200 swans which fed on the Exe and other estuaries in Devon. This study revealed seasonal variation in methods of feeding and in food plants selected. In spring and early summer, the swans grazed on the saltmarsh turf, selecting the succulents, sea arrowgrass *Triglochin maritima* and sea plantain *Plantago maritima*; common saltmarsh-grass (sea poa) *Puccinellia maritima* was the favourite grass. During July and August the flocks moved to the estuary, where they fed on eel-grass *Zostera* and a green alga *Enteromorpha*. In the late autumn and winter, the swans fed either on nearby marshes or on the river at Exeter, where they also obtained bread from the public.

The stomachs from eight Mute Swans from the Ouse Washes were examined by Owen and Cadbury (1975). The results of this study, together with observations from the same area, showed the major foods to be the soft grasses: marsh foxtail *Alopecurus geniculatus*, creeping bent *Agrostis stolonifera* and floating sweet-grass *Glyceria fluitans*. In addition, starchy roots of marsh yellow-cress *Rorippa islandica* were taken, as were aquatic plants such as water-starwort *Callitriche*, soft hornwort *Ceratophyllum demersum* and water-crowfoot *Ranunculus*.

The swans at Abbotsbury also depend largely on *Zostera* and to a lesser extent *Ruppia*. Although these die down to some extent during the late winter, the swans almost always seem to have sufficient for their needs; at least, they rarely come out and feed on the fields which line the Fleet. The most serious damage to the food supply is done by the weather. Strong winds may uproot much of the *Zostera* and kill it, or ice may freeze it, making it useless for the swans. In harsh winters, the birds may encounter food shortages and suffer higher mortality than usual. In most years, however, the food supply is not only sufficient for the needs of the local swans, but many others may come in and feed.

This is about the limit of our knowledge on the food of the Mute Swan in Britain. To supplement this, we have to rely on information from studies in Sweden and Denmark (Spärck 1957, Brenneke 1962, Berglund *et al.* 1963, Luther 1963, Olsson 1963). These studies arose because there was thought to be a conflict between swans and local fishing interests. Consequently, large numbers of swans were shot in some of these studies to determine their diet.

One Swedish study took place along the southeast coast and islands around Karlskrona, between 1957 and 1962 (Berglund *et al.* 1963). Forty-five stomachs were examined during the spring and summer months, and they were seen to contain mainly stonewort *Chara* species;

green algae *Enteromorpha* and *Cladophora*, beaked tasselweed (wigeon grass) *Ruppia maritima* and the brown alga *Pylaiella rupurcola* were also taken earlier in the year. Another Swedish study which took place some 200km to the north, on a brackish-water inlet, relied on analysis of droppings and examination of uprooted vegetation left behind by the feeding swans (Olsson 1963). The main food items included *Potamogeton*, water-milfoil *Myriophyllum* and the green algae *Cladophora* and *Vaucheria*.

The Danish study (Spärck 1957), which took place around the coast of Zealand, was based on examination of around 70 stomachs collected between October and June. The main food types were *Zostera, Ruppia, Potamogeton* and *Chara* and seven-horned pondweed *Zannichellia pedunculata*.

All these studies concluded that Mute Swans feed almost exclusively on plant matter. They also indicate the importance of a wide variety of vegetation types. Small amounts of animal matter, however, are taken, presumably often caught up in the swans' vegetable food. Animals taken in this way include frogs, toads, tadpoles, worms, crustaceans, insects and molluscs (Cramp and Simmons 1977). Occasionally, swans are reported eating fish, but this is most irregular (Hulme 1948, Goethe 1965, Scott *et al.* 1972). Anglers have also said that swans can eat large quantities of fish spawn, but it seems that, if they do this at all, they do so only by accident while they are eating vegetation.

Food Demands

The amount of food a swan requires depends on the time of year and the age of the particular individual. For mature adult swans, the maximum demand for food increases as the bird approaches the breeding season. Females are at their heaviest just prior to egg-laying (Reynolds 1972), some putting on as much as 2kg in weight at this time of year. Three females were weighed just before they laid their first egg, and they all weighed in excess of 11kg, as opposed to the normal 9-9.5kg for female Mute Swans. Clearly, females have to be in prime condition when forming eggs, as the production of six or more eggs, each weighing around 300g, is energetically very expensive. In addition, they also need to lay down fat reserves for the long incubation period. During this critical time the male guards the female, allowing her to feed undisturbed on the best territory he can find and defend. During laying, the male may sit on the eggs and defend them, allowing the female to spend the maximum amount of time feeding. The male appears to go quite long periods without feeding during the egg-laying period. Clearly, the male, too, needs to be in good condition and well fed before the start of this period, as ultimately he has to defend the territory. Once the clutch is complete, the female starts incubating and the male has more time to feed.

During the five-week incubation period, the female hardly feeds at all, and is dependent on the food reserves (fat) which she laid down prior to egg-laying. By the end of incubation, the female has used up almost all her stored reserves and has lost over 1kg in weight. She feeds very little at this time, and occasionally incubation may go on for longer than the usual 35 days. In certain parts of the country where game-fishing is popular, we have come across eggs in which someone has made small holes so that they will not hatch. It takes an awful lot to put off a female swan from incubating her eggs, and she will push herself to the very edge of survival in this situation. The instinct to incubate is so strong that not until she is on the point of starving will the female leave her eggs.

The type of food available to a pair of swans and their cygnets on their territory affects their reproductive performance. Dafila Scott (Scott and Birkhead 1983) examined food availability on the River Thames and its tributaries, the Thame, the Cherwell and the Windrush. Four measures of food quality on the territories were used: (i) the amount and (ii) the diversity of aquatic vegetation in the territory; (iii) the potential amount of bread supplied by the public, and (iv) the amount of accessible pasture for grazing. Scott then compared these measures with measures of breeding performance such as clutch-size, laying date, egg volume, the number of cygnets fledged and the weight of the young at the end of August.

There was a great deal of variation in the amount of, and the types of, food available on the different territories. It was difficult to determine how much vegetation was available to the swans, so a specially designed double-headed rake was used to sample the vegetation; this was dragged through the water on a rope and the resulting sample of vegetation weighed. Although this worked quite well, it was difficult explaining to inquisitive passers-by what was going on! On territories with abundant aquatic vegetation, females laid their eggs earlier and had larger clutches than those on territories with little aquatic vegetation. Bread supplied by the public was also important, and clutches were larger on territories with a greater bread supply. The weight of the breeding female was related to the diversity of aquatic plants on a territory: the greater the diversity, the heavier the female. Clearly, the food available to a breeding pair has an important effect on some aspects of their breeding performance, but we did not find any significant relationships between measures of territory quality and other aspects of breeding performance, such as the number of cygnets raised.

Other critical times when food requirements are high include (i) the period before the annual moult and (ii) periods of harsh weather. Mute Swans have been known to lose nearly 1 kg in weight (about 10 per cent of their body weight) during the 4-7-week moult period. During harsh weather, a swan has to rely on its body reserves as large quantities of these are burnt to keep warm.

Very little work has been carried out on the actual quantity of food a swan consumes, but one estimate suggests a daily consumption of around 4 kg (wet weight) of vegetation (Mathiasson 1973). Doubtless this will vary with the circumstances.

Cygnets and Food

Young swans hatch with a fairly good supply of food in their yolk sacs, on which they can live for several days (Kear 1965, Lack 1968). In that time they have got to learn to feed themselves, as their parents do not

Plate 17. A family of cygnets feeds on pondweed in a quiet backwater in Oxfordshire

actually put food in their mouths as do many other bird species. The cygnets are not, however, totally independent of their parents, since the adult birds perform a number of vital functions for their young: firstly, they protect them from potential predators; secondly, they will brood their young in very cold or wet conditions, which keeps them warm and helps them to conserve heat and energy; thirdly, they help to make food more available to their cygnets. The parents stir up food by foot-paddling so that the youngsters can peck at the surface, picking up small food items; they will also bring up food from below the water surface which would otherwise be out of reach of the cygnets. In addition, the adults will lead their family to good feeding areas, which, in some cases, may involve a journey of several miles.

Two particular family excursions, associated with moving to areas of good feeding for the cygnets, spring to mind from our studies of the Oxford birds (see also page 102). The first family was known as the 'Wolfson Pair', because we often found them in the Wolfson College punt harbour. They usually nested, however, nearby in the University parks. This was one of our favourite pairs of swans and the male was the biggest swan in the study area, weighing in at 16kg! This heavyweight of a swan not only chased off all other swans from the area, but he also gave punters, and dogs and their masters, a hard time. He undoubtedly had the freedom of the River Cherwell and, each year after his cygnets had hatched, he took them almost 5km upriver to a rich feeding area near Islip. To do this, he had to pass through at least two other swan territories, but no other male could stop him. The area where he took his family, presumably an excellent feeding area, was a shallow stretch of river with abundant water-crowfoot.

The second journey was not confined to the rivers. The particular pair involved bred on a lake on the outskirts of Oxford. Once the cygnets had hatched, they moved from the lake to a canal and then onto the River Thames, and from there to Seacourt stream, a tributary of the Thames. One of the most daring parts of the excursion, from the lake to the canal, however, involved crossing a railway line. Once again, the area they made for was a shallow stretch of river with large floating mats of crowfoot.

Feeding Development

The development of feeding techniques in cygnets follows a more or less set pattern. Initially the parents 'stir', or pull up the food for the chicks, who, in turn, peck at the pieces on the surface of the water. Alternatively, they filter the water surface: a less subtle but more efficient way of collecting what is on the surface. By the time a cygnet is a week old, however, it can already submerge its whole head for about two seconds (Dewar 1942). This ability to submerge gradually increases to six seconds after four weeks and only to $7\frac{1}{2}$ seconds after 60 days.

The more tricky business of 'up-ending' starts at about ten days, but it takes several weeks of practice for the cygnets to get it right. By the time the swan is two weeks old, it can actually pull up its own vegetation and food rather than indiscriminately pecking at the water surface.

Plate 18. The parents will often pull up vegetation from the lake or river bottom for their expectant and hungry young

Some work has been carried out on food selection by really young cygnets (Kear 1964). It is clear that they select their food items at first mainly by eye; this seems reasonable, as they feed exclusively on the water surface at this stage. Basically, cygnets will peck at almost anything they see moving on the water, but it appears that they have a preference for green and yellow objects — perhaps the prominent colour of available vegetation? As the cygnets age, and feed more underwater, selection may depend partly on taste and touch, but there are few data on this at present.

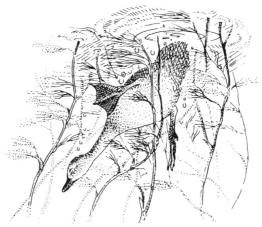

Young cygnets will occasionally dive below the water surface in search of food

Food from the Public

Mute Swans, particularly those in urban flocks, are virtually semi-domesticated and survive to a large extent on food from the public. Most of the food is usually bread, but we have come across people who provide a wide range of food types — from Brussels sprouts to crisps and peanuts. In the case of peanuts, it is difficult to know whether the swans are selecting food or looking for pieces of grit! These urban flocks represent quite a sizeable proportion of the British Mute Swan population and, since they contain most of the next generation of breeders, they are very important to the well-being of the population. It is almost certain that, when the Mute Swan population was very high during the late 1950s (see Chapter 3), the supplementary food provided by the public was very important in times of food shortage, such as at the end of winter. Not all the food the swans obtained from man was intended for them; large flocks of swans were regularly attracted to waste grain spills from mills and distilleries. There were a number of well-known sites along the Lower Thames, at Mistley in Essex and at Burton-on-Trent, but most of these sources of food and the large aggregations that collected at them have since disappeared.

In some localities along the River Thames, certain flocks or individual swans will visit their hosts regularly. Once a pattern is established, it is not uncommon for the swans, like 'Henry' at Goring Lock, to waddle up to a door or window and peck at it to demand his 'daily bread'. One lady in Marlow used to feed a pair of swans on bread and Grand Marnier! Another lady in the Henley-on-Thames area provided vast quantities of bread and green vegetables for a flock of 20 swans. It is this kind of relationship between swans and humans that has kept swans so tame.

Mute Swans are quite happy to accept 'hand-outs' from the public

Do Swans Cause Damage?

There have been a number of complaints about swans causing damage. For the most part, the serious complaints are from anglers who blame swans for eating fish spawn and from farmers who claim damage to crops.

Damage to Fishing Interests

Anglers have been concerned for some considerable time about the damage to fish stocks from swans eating fish spawn. For example, Stevenson (1890) quotes a report in *Land and Water* for 30 November 1872 of a petition by the Great Marlow Thames Angling Association to the Lord Chamberlain 'praying for a reduction in the number of the Queen's swans on the Thames ... on the ground of the injury done to the fishing by these birds in the consumption of fish spawn'. In 1929, the Thames Angling Preservation Society wrote to the Lord Chamberlain's Office about 'the damage done to Thames Angling by destruction of fish fry and spawn by swans and other water fowl'. They also referred to earlier complaints dating back to the beginning of the century.

One of the claims was that the birds were doing particular damage to perch stocks. Perch lay their eggs in long ribbons and, so it was claimed, the swans would find and consume a whole ribbon — of 120,000-280,000 eggs — within minutes. These ribbons are laid around twigs and water plants. Curiously, it was said at the time that the swans were not affecting the stocks of roach, which lay large quantities of sticky, but separate eggs which adhere to the water plants. It seems most improbable that this complaint is justified. Swans do not normally feed on anything other than vegetable material and would be most unlikely to take fry, simply because they would be unable to catch them. They might affect a small quantity of the fish spawn indirectly by eating the water plants; while doing so, they undoubtedly would swallow any eggs attached to the plants. This is, however, unlikely to have any important effect on the fish stocks, since the fry compete with one another for food, and even a heavy loss of eggs is not likely to affect the eventual stock of fish; this will depend on the food supply available to them.

Only one detailed study of the possible effects of swans on fish stocks has been undertaken. This was carried out in Sweden (Berglund *et al.* 1963), and showed conclusively that the birds had no effect on the fish stocks; at the most, they might have been responsible for creating certain open areas of water within large areas of weeds, but even these might have been brought about by the action of ice in the winter. They even killed 13 swans during the peak spawning time for pike and perch, but found no spawn in their stomachs.

If for some reason the stock of water plants is very low in a particular river, as now seems to be the case in many lowland rivers, then the possibility exists that the fish and the swans both want the same plants, but for different reasons. If the stock of plants falls so low that there is insufficient, then competition from the swans may lead to a significant loss of spawning grounds; even this, however, seems unlikely, since many of the fish can, and do, spawn around the fine underwater roots of trees or on plants in water too deep for swans to reach.

Nor is the vegetation eaten by the swans totally lost to the system. It is soon returned and, especially in lakes where it is not slowly washed downstream, the droppings provide a rich source of food for the tiny animals that are themselves the food of fish fry. In Poland, it seems to be widely held that these droppings enhance the lake nutrients and provide good water for fish spawning. Sokolowski (1960) points out that:

'It is not by accident that Lake Lukniany, harbouring hundreds of swans has become famous as the spawning grounds of the bream and other fish of commercial value. All neighbouring lakes connected with Lake Lukniany by water are stocked with the fry of the bream derived from that lake.'

In some areas, swans have been recommended for opening areas in very weedy waters so that the waters can be fished. Naumann and Naumann (1905) quote instances of German lakes becoming totally overgrown after the swans were removed. Stevenson (1890) quotes a record of the Marquis of Exeter successfully using two pairs of swans to keep open parts of a sheet of water overrun with weeds.

Undoubtedly, on a well-vegetated stream, a few swans will not seriously damage the stocks of water plants and so will certainly not interfere with spawning fish. We cannot, however, say that a large flock on a restricted area of water plants would never do any damage. We know of one stretch of river where the anglers have realised that they can put the swans' own behaviour to good use. By permitting a pair of swans to nest and raise their cygnets unmolested, they have provided themselves with the best possible insurance against an accumulation of moulting non-breeders; the territorial cob takes good care that such an unwanted gathering never happens on *his* stretch of river!

Damage to Farming

Some of the complaints by farmers are more valid. Swans do settle on agricultural fields. Complaints are most frequent in late winter and early spring, the time, of course, when natural foods are scarcest. Swans may settle on early-winter cereals. Nor are they stupid; they often select the most advanced crop in the neighbourhood, thereby angering the farmer, who is just priding himself on having got a crop which is ahead of those of his neighbours. They also may go on to improved pastures and make themselves unpopular by competing with the grazing animals for the 'first bite', again at a time when the farmer is anxious to get his animals out on to the fields so as to avoid having to go on providing fodder at that time of year when food is at its most expensive. Swans may also be unpopular if they settle in an area for the moult in midsummer. The difficulty for them — and the farmer — is that once they have moulted they cannot go far until the new flight feathers have grown; they have no option but to stay.

Swans not only graze, but their large feet flatten quite a lot of grass and they also foul the fields. The damage done is, of course, immeasurably small on a national scale, but can be aggravating to any one particular farmer (Eltringham 1963b).

It is difficult to assess the actual financial damage. When the birds are eating the leaves of winter cereals, the long-term effect seems to be almost negligible, especially if one takes into account the fact that the birds refertilise the field. If the swans are allowed to remain on the field

Mute Swans will graze on grass and winter cereals

long enough to be able to take or trample down the fruiting stalk, however, then damage is clearly done, as is the case with the fouling of the first bite on grazing land. More rarely, Mute Swans have been recorded walking into mature grain fields and taking the grain from the standing crop. In one such case, on oats, a pair plus four cygnets caused considerable damage to part of a field (Harle 1951).

Stopping the swans from being a nuisance is becoming progressively more difficult as the amount of other feeding for them diminishes, a point we shall return to later (page 147). It is sometimes possible to keep a moulting flock off a field in midsummer, simply by erecting short stretches of wire netting along the riverbank. Since the birds cannot fly at this stage, only the areas of bank where they can walk out need to be covered; this strategy has been successful on a number of occasions.

Birds that have taken a liking to a field in late winter are more difficult to deter. One of the difficulties here is that farmers are often rather slow to deter them, and so the swans build up a habit which they are not willing to change. The main difficulty seems to be that many farmers quite like swans; certainly they do not consider that a pair of them on a field does any serious damage. Hence, the first birds to arrive are left alone. Other swans flying in the vicinity soon see the two birds down in the field, regard the field as safe and desirable, and descend to join them. The result is that what may have started out as a single pair may soon build up to 30 or 40 birds. While they are off the actual water, the swans do not seem to be very aggressive and so even a local, established, territorial pair makes little attempt to chase the others off (though they may well do so if the birds get onto the river). The real solution seems to be that, if the field is one which the farmer particularly wants to remain swan-free, then he should be quick to chase off the first arrivals and not allow them to settle in.

CHAPTER
7
Causes of Mortality

Although, because they are so conspicuous, many dead Mute Swans are found, it is difficult to be confident about the importance of the different causes of death as most estimates are open to bias of one sort or another. In this chapter, we shall look at some of these estimates and discuss the biases most likely to affect them. We first examine the causes of death of ringed birds reported to the British Trust for Ornithology (BTO); we shall then look at some of the causes of death, finishing with a more detailed review of lead poisoning.

Analyses of British Trust for Ornithology Records

At the end of the 1970s when the Nature Conservancy Council set up a working party to investigate lead poisoning and the causes of mortality in Mute Swans (NCC 1981), there was little information about what killed the birds. Most of what was available stemmed from recoveries of dead swans which had been ringed.

These data are likely to contain certain biases. Only about one-third of the swans which are ringed are later found dead and reported. Dead swans are much more likely to be found if they die in the vicinity of man. For example, every swan which is killed in a collision with a power or telephone line leads to a power or telephone failure and consequently the dead swan will probably be found by the repair man. Thus, ringing-recovery data have a bias towards areas with a relatively high human population, where dead birds have a greater chance of being found.

Of 3,783 ringed Mute Swans reported dead, no cause of death was given in 2,110 (56 per cent) of the cases (Table 7.1). Another bias is that, where a cause of death was given, this was based on a casual observation by a member of the public and therefore only conspicuous causes of death were recognised.

Both these biases are apparent from Table 7.1. By far the commonest identified cause of death is collisions with overhead power cables (809 cases, or 21 per cent). Clearly, there is a strong bias in favour of causes of death which produce obvious external injuries. Less obvious causes of death, such as disease, parasite infestation, and poisoning, cannot be detected by the casual observer.

Table 7.1: Causes of death in the Mute Swan, based on reports of recoveries of ringed birds

Cause of death				No.	%
Collisions	(i)	Overhead wires	809		
	(ii)	Bridges	53		
	(iii)	Road casualties	95		
	(iv)	Railway accidents	37		
		TOTAL =		994	26.3
Killed by animals				228	6.0
Killed by man	(i)	Shot	123		
	(ii)	Fish hooks, line	42		
		TOTAL =		165	4.4
Oil				238	6.3
Miscellaneous				48	1.3
No cause of death given				2,110	55.7
Overall total				3,783	100.0

From Perrins (1981)

The Causes of Death

Collisions

The most common cause of death, as determined by this analysis, was collisions with man-made objects (26 per cent). Previous analyses of ringing recoveries carried out in the mid-1960s (Ogilvie 1967) showed that 44 per cent of reported swan deaths were due to collisions.

While swans of all ages die from collisions, the immature birds, as opposed to the young (cygnets) and the mature (adults), seem to suffer the highest mortality. These are the birds that are most actively searching for breeding territories and such losses seem to be heaviest in spring and autumn, the times when they are seeking out their new territories (see also Figure 5.1). There is no evidence that the older swans have got

Hundreds of swans die each year as a result of collisions with overhead power cables

to know the position of certain obstacles in their area, although we cannot be sure that they do not do so. Rather, mortality from collisions seems to reflect the activity of swans.

It is not altogether surprising that swans experience such high mortality from flying accidents, as they are large, heavy birds that, once they get going, fly at speeds of 30-50 mph (50-80 kph). In addition, they have only average eyesight with poor forward vision. Slender objects such as power lines will obviously cause problems, especially when visibility is poor. Individuals and flocks frequently collide with power lines; sometimes the impact is enough to kill the swans, and sometimes they are electrocuted. The worst collision of which we have heard concerns eight swans which simultaneously flew into a length of cable along the Thames Valley. Another report, from Kent, referred to 21 swans dying along one stretch of power line within a period of two months (Harrison 1963).

Markers, such as brightly coloured balls, along the wires can reduce the casualty rate, and in a very few areas they have been fitted. Accidents of the sort mentioned, however, are not infrequent and more could be done with advantage in this field. Since the collisions can result in serious damage or inconvenience to power consumers, we should have thought it worthwhile to try to make more lines clearly visible. We know of at least one little village in Oxfordshire being blacked out for several hours because a swan broke the power line. Other countries have reflectors or similar devices along their power lines, but as yet these are not widespread in Britain.

Vandals and Shooting

A number of Mute Swans are killed each year by vandals, including being shot with air-rifles and crossbows. We do not know what proportion of deaths occur illegally in this way, but if, as we suppose, some of the birds are removed and eaten then no evidence will remain on the river, and the importance of this factor will remain under-recorded. Particularly sickening are some of the cases in which incubating birds are killed by repeated blows from bricks, bottles and other missiles. Not only is a breeding adult destroyed, but the whole clutch is lost, too. The incidence of vandalism varies from area to area, but it is particularly high in the Midlands.

Oiling

Discharge of oil, although illegal, is still a real problem. In fact, as we are writing this chapter, it has just been reported that over 100 Mute Swans at Berwick-upon-Tweed have been badly oiled: 2,000 gallons (10,000 litres) of heavy industrial oil were released into the river by vandals, killing over 50 swans; a further 100 swans were taken off the river by the RSPCA for treatment. The river was so badly oiled that many swans had to be shot on the water, and a local RSPCA inspector described the swans as looking like 'ebony statues' as they were taken out. There have been numerous other incidents around the country, but the worst seems to have been one that occurred at Burton-upon-Trent in the Midlands when 85 birds died out of a flock of 100 (Scott *et al.* 1972).

Oil kills swans either through their ingesting it, which results in severe enteritis, or through damaging their waterproofing. Once the feather's

Oiling is still a major problem for waterbirds, especially the Mute Swan

own protective coating of preen oil has been damaged, water will get through the feathers and the bird will soon die of exposure. Oiled birds try to clean their feathers, but if they swallow oil they may be poisoned. If an oiled bird is caught early enough and taken into care, where it is fed and kept warm, it can, however, often be cleaned and make a full recovery, but it takes time to clean the feathers and allow the swan to regain its normal waterproofing.

Predation

Losses from predation are hard to quantify and highlight another difficulty in ascertaining the true cause of death. A swan may have actually died at the hands of a predator, but it may have already been sick or injured from a completely different cause. Yet the reported cause of death will be predation. For example, 228 of the recoveries of ringed Mute Swans record that the bird was killed by a predator such as a fox or sometimes a dog. Although it is possible that a fox may successfully kill an incubating female swan, we rather doubt that it happens very often. At other times it seems even more unlikely that a fox could catch a healthy swan, since the birds are normally on open water or in the middle of open fields. We suspect that many of the swans reported as killed by foxes either were very sick and so were on the riverbank and easily caught, or were already dead and merely found and eaten by a fox. Certainly, dead swans beneath power lines are often quickly found and eaten by foxes, though they obviously died as a result of the collision. Apart from man and foxes, and perhaps mink and pike where very small cygnets are concerned, the Mute Swan has few enemies in Britain, although in Poland swans have been killed by wolves and their nests raided by wild boar.

Death from Natural Causes

There are a number of causes of mortality which can be considered under the heading of 'natural causes'. Cold weather is thought to be a major killer only in very severe winters, such as the one of 1962/63. Strictly, the birds do not usually die because of the low temperatures; their feathers are excellent insulators, as anyone who sleeps in an all-feather duvet will know. The usual problem is that low temperatures cause lakes and rivers to freeze over and make the food inaccessible. If the cold lasts long enough, the swan may die of starvation.

Mute Swans, like a number of other wildfowl, seem to be prone to numerous diseases and a detailed review is presented in Scott *et al.* (1972). Viral and bacterial diseases are relatively common in the Mute Swan, and in recent years a common problem has been with botulism, which is caused by a botulinum-type C toxin. The bacterium concerned, *Clostridium botulinum*, thrives in shallow water, especially in warm weather. It can be a serious problem in hot, dry summers, when the rivers expose large expanses of mud. Because tissue samples taken prior to death are required in order to prove conclusively that the bird was suffering from botulism, this proof is rarely achieved. Consequently, it is quite likely that botulism is under-recorded. We have also come across tuberculosis in two swans from the River Thames.

Mute Swans have their fair share of ectoparasites and endoparasites. Recently, a study of heartworm (*Sarconema eurycerca*) by S. Cohen at Loughborough University of Technology has raised the possibility that this might cause death in some swans. At the moment, however, there is no evidence that this is the case. Of 37 swans tested from the River Thames, none had heartworm. At Abbotsbury, Dorset, although 42 per cent of the birds tested had heartworm, these swans have the highest survival rate in Britain!

If you are a swan catcher, or have ever handled swans, you will almost certainly be familiar with their feather lice, Mallophaga, which manage to get in your hair however hard you try to prevent them. These are quite large lice, about 5-10 mm in length, with a flat profile and are extremely difficult to squash. They feed on skin and feather debris and, although most individuals have a few of them, if a swan becomes ill and cannot preen, the numbers of lice may increase and affect the condition of its plumage, leading to a diminution in the bird's health.

Swans can also contract fungal diseases such as aspergillosis, the most important agent of which seems to be *Aspergillus fumigatus*. This fungus causes severe respiratory problems which often lead to death. The disease is particularly common among young birds and individuals under stress.

Thousands of swans die every year through ingesting anglers' discarded lead weights

Lead Poisoning: the background

As we can see from Table 7.1, in well over half the cases where ringed Mute Swans were reported dead, no cause of death was given and, in some of those where a cause was given, that cause is fairly suspect and may well not be the ultimate factor which led to the swan's death. In other words, the majority of dead swans have no obvious, external cause of death; they have died from a cause that cannot be determined easily by the casual observer.

When we started our study of the causes of death on the Thames, we already knew that swans were prone to die from lead poisoning. Conse-quently, this was an obvious factor to look for. Many species of wildfowl are known to suffer lead poisoning through the ingestion of lead gun-shot. Most of our knowledge comes from the United States of America, where it has been known to be a major factor in mortality of wildfowl for over a century (Phillips and Lincoln 1930). The problem was first recorded as long ago as the 1800s in Italy (Sebastiano and Delprato 1880). Today, lead poisoning resulting from the ingestion of spent gun-shot has been confirmed in 15 countries (Thomas 1980), and extensive research has been carried out in Britain on the incidence and signifi-cance of ingested lead-pellet poisoning in wildfowl (Mudge 1983).

In 1973, 18 Mute Swans were found dead or dying on the River Trent. Examination at post-mortem revealed that 16 of these birds had died from lead poisoning due to ingesting anglers' discarded lead weights (Simpson *et al.* 1979). The majority of those weights are the 'split-shot' which the anglers attach to their lines to weight the float. This was the first published record of swans, or indeed of any wildfowl, dying from such a cause. We have been told, however, that in 1963 a small number of dead Thames swans were found to have high levels of lead in their tissues; the work was carried out by the Ministry of Agriculture, Fisheries and Food (MAFF), but it was neither published nor followed up. One other study (Owen and Cadbury 1975) collected 37 dead swans from the Ouse Washes in East Anglia between 1969 and 1975; 29 per cent were found to have died from lead poisoning and most of these birds had ingested anglers' lead weights.

How Do Swans Die from Lead Poisoning?

Swans, like most other birds, have no teeth with which to grind up their food. They grind it up in their large muscular gizzard (a bird's stomach), using grit — small pieces of gravel — to help them. The grit, the sharp edges of which help to break down the cellulose plant walls, also gets worn down and needs to be replaced frequently. As a result, swans have to search for grit regularly. They pick up and swallow any hard grit-like substances which they come across, and this includes lead weights if they are there. Consequently, these weights enter the gizzard and, being soft, are ground down with the grit. The lead is released into the gizzard and eventually absorbed into the blood stream, and so finds its way into other tissues.

Dabbling in the mud. A Mute Swan will inadvertently pick up lost lead weights while searching for grit and gravel to fill its gizzard

Plate 19. A healthy adult swan with a straight neck

Plate 20. A lead-poisoned adult swan with its characteristic 'kinked' neck

Plate 21. The lead-poisoned cygnet (far right) is easily discernible by the shape of its neck

Any ingested lead characteristically affects the neuromuscular system. Humans with lead poisoning suffer from 'floppy wrists', and swans get 'kinky necks'; the neck muscles are weakened such that a swan is unable to maintain its usual upright posture. The most obvious signs internally of lead poisoning are often an oesophagus (gullet) packed with food; the lead inhibits the usual rhythmic muscular contractions that propel food through the gut. The end result is that the swan dies of starvation even though its gullet may be packed with food (Birkhead 1982).

Although it has yet to be proved in the case of swans, sub-lethal doses of lead could have an adverse effect on certain behaviours, particularly those which require a high degree of co-ordination and skill, such as courtship and flying. Cattle poisoned by lead commonly become blind (Clarke and Clarke 1975) and, since a large number of swans die each year through collisions with objects such as overhead power cables, it remains possible that lead poisoning may lead to deaths in flying accidents.

Post-mortem Analyses

Over the last few years, between 2,000 and 3,000 Mute Swans have been examined at post-mortem (NCC 1981, Birkhead 1982, French in prep.). At the time of the national inquiry into lead poisoning in swans (NCC 1981), 327 and 72 swans respectively from the Midlands and the River Thames had been autopsied. The 327 from the Midlands had been collected during the years 1973 to 1980, and 50.4 per cent had died as a result of lead poisoning. In certain parts of the Midlands, the problem was more acute; 90 per cent of swans examined from the River Trent and 77 per cent from Stratford-upon-Avon had died from this cause. On the River Thames, 75 per cent had died from lead poisoning, and the severity of the problem increased downstream towards London.

No swan was confirmed as having died from lead poisoning unless detailed analyses of its body organs showed it to contain highly elevated lead levels; such levels normally coincided with the presence of split lead shot in the bird's gizzard (Table 7.2). Of the swans examined which were diagnosed as having died from lead poisoning, 69 per cent of the Thames birds, 85 per cent of those from East Anglia, and 90 per cent of those examined by the Veterinary Investigation Centre, Loughborough, still had pieces of lead in their gizzard. On average, the number of lead weights found in a lead-poisoned swan is around seven.

Since the national inquiry of 1981, many more swans have been autopsied. Table 7.3 shows the results of three different sets of post-mortem analyses. The study by the Institute of Terrestrial Ecology (ITE) relates primarily to East Anglia, the MAFF data are countrywide, and the Oxford study covers most of the Thames drainage area (excluding Gloucestershire). As before, the proportion of the dead birds which have died from lead poisoning remains very high. Overall, more swans are dying from this cause than from any other. Indeed, in many areas, more Mute Swans are dying from lead poisoning than from all other causes of death added together.

Table 7.2: Tissue lead levels in micrograms (µg)/100ml of blood, weight of, and number of shot found in the gizzard of, two categories of dead Mute Swans (lead-poisoned, and dying from other causes)

Cause of death	Median lead level (µg/100ml) Liver	Kidney	Mean weight (kg)	Mean number lead shot
Lead poisoning	105	908	5.7	7.0
(range)	10-562	105-5,225		0-28
	(n=51)	(n=50)	(n=48)	(n=53)
Other than lead poisoning	4	8	8.9	0
(range)	1-22	1-116		
	(n=39)	(n=37)	(n=30)	(n=39)

From Birkhead (1982)

Table 7.3: Proportion of Mute Swans dying of lead poisoning

ITE analyses* (M. French in prep.)

	Oct. 81-Sept. 82	Oct. 82-Sept. 83	Oct. 83 to date
Total post-mortems	320	186	121
No. lead-poisoned	228	139	94
% lead-poisoned	71.2	74.7	77.7

MAFF analyses** (A. Hunt pers. comm.)

	1982	1983	1984
Total post-mortems	254	240	172
No. lead-poisoned	123	127	73
% lead-poisoned	48.4	52.9	42.4

Oxford study (J. Sears pers. comm.)

	Jan. 82-Sept. 84
Total post-mortems	284
No. lead-poisoned	159
% lead-poisoned	56.0

* These figures will slightly overestimate the deaths from *angling weights*. In 392 cases where the lead weights were identified, 6 (1.5%) were gunshot.
**These figures are for England only. The figures for the four years from 1981 to present are: Wales, 6/18 (33%); and Scotland, 22/162 (13.6%).

In recent years, there has been a lot of publicity about the dangers of lead, and anglers have been encouraged not to discard their lead weights. Hence, it is particularly important to know whether or not the situation is improving. There is, however, no indication to suppose that it is getting any better. The slightly reduced percentage of deaths from lead poisoning in the 1984 MAFF inquiries seems to result from an increase in deaths due to botulism during the prolonged hot summer, rather than a reduction in the numbers dying from lead poisoning.

There remain strong regional differences in the occurrence of lead poisoning. Few birds die from this cause in Scotland, whereas the percentage dying from lead in the Midlands, East Anglia and the Lower Thames is exceptionally high, in excess of 60 per cent. Deaths from lead poisoning on the River Tames in total are slightly lower than on the Trent, but this is because the Thames study includes a number of small tributaries, such as the Windrush, Thame and Cherwell, and the quiet Upper Thames. The Lower Thames itself, below Windsor, however, has one of the highest incidences of lead poisoning in the country, in excess of 80 per cent.

In certain areas around the country, the figures quoted today – as opposed to three years ago – probably underestimate the 'natural' frequency of lead poisoning, since many sick birds are now taken into care and treated by organisations such as 'Save our Swans' on the River Thames and 'Swansave' in East Anglia. Without these organisations, the proportion dying from lead poisoning would undoubtedly be higher.

The Age of Ingested Lead Weights

Although swans may pick up lead when searching for grit in the river sediments, we think that many may pick up these weights in another way. On the River Thames in particular, the evidence supports the suggestion that many of the lead weights picked up by the swans are ones that have been recently lost or discarded (Birkhead 1983). We suspect that at least some of these birds have picked up a piece of line with a set of weights attached. This ties in both with post-mortem results, which show that more swans die of lead poisoning during the summer months when coarse angling is at its most popular (Birkhead 1982), and with the studies of lead levels in live swans (see next section). Also, out of 35 swans suffering from lead poisoning which were taken into care at Windsor during 1984, all but four had more than one lead weight in their gizzard; the other 31 had a total of 214 weights (average of about seven per bird), the maximum in any one individual being 24. It remains a puzzle as to how the birds gather so many lead weights unless they take them in on line.

Further evidence that many of the lead weights are ones that have been recently lost comes from some of the gravel-pits where fishing has only of late been permitted. At one pond near Coalville, Leicestershire, there was no fishing until the water was stocked and opened to angling in June 1983; within two months, a swan died of lead poisoning – with eight split lead shot in its gizzard. At a lake at Melbourne Hall, Derbyshire, there had been no fishing before June 1982; three swans died of lead poisoning within six months of fishing starting, and a fourth died in early 1983.

We believe that this information is important because it indicates that, although doubtless swans will continue to die of lead poisoning for many years to come, there might be rapid improvement in the situation if lead could be withdrawn.

Lead Levels in Living Swans

Although post-mortems show the impact of lead poisoning, in certain areas — especially on the Thames, where numbers are now small — it is difficult to obtain enough data. Consequently, in order to assess the effects of poisoning on the Thames, we monitored lead levels in the blood of live birds (Birkhead 1983).

Studies on lead levels in the blood of other wildfowl (Cook and Trainer 1966, Roscoe 1978) indicated that a level of over 40 micrograms of lead per 100 millilitres of blood (40 µg per 100 ml) meant that the bird had suffered from lead poisoning at some time during its life or was just getting a dose. We checked this in Mute Swans by looking at the blood from 100 individuals at Abbotsbury, where we were fairly sure that there was no problem from lead poisoning. Every bird had a blood lead level below 40 micrograms per 100 millilitres of blood.

Over the last few years, thousands of blood samples have been taken from swans on the River Thames and its tributaries, with some individuals being sampled several times in a lifetime. The results of these studies showed that many swans were 'over the limit'. In general, lead levels increased with proximity to London, while swans on the tributaries tended to have lower blood lead levels.

Swans are not the only birds to show an increase in blood lead levels with proximity to London. This phenomenon was also demonstrated for feral pigeons, *Columba livia* (Hutton 1980). Hutton suggested that this was due to an increase in ingesting food contaminated with roadside dust. This is unlikely to be the case with the Mute Swan. It seems prob-

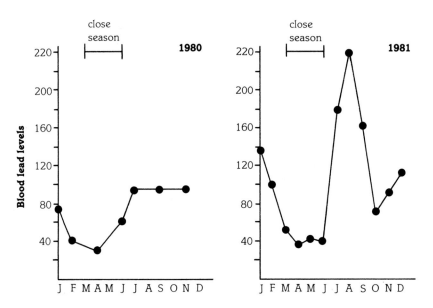

Figure 7.1: Monthly median blood lead levels (µg/100 ml) from a flock of Mute Swans at Reading on the River Thames

From Birkhead (1983)

able that there would be a slight increase in the background level of lead in the river as one gets nearer to London. The increase in blood lead levels of flock birds with proximity to London probably reflects an increase in fishing and particularly in available lead weights. These urban swans may be prone to lead poisoning for a number of reasons. One is that lead weights lost in these areas remain available on the concrete wharfs and embankments, whereas the weights lost in the countryside are more likely to be lost in the mud and on the grassy banks. It is possible that boating may also add to the problem by stirring up the sediment which contains lead weights; and, as the river is tidal at places such as Richmond, weights lost on the banks may get washed into the shallows following high tide.

One of the most important results from the investigation into blood lead levels among the flock birds showed that their levels were at their highest during the coarse-angling season, and it was only during the close season that levels dropped to around 40 μg per 100 ml of blood (Figure 7.1). This supports the idea that swans are picking up recently discarded lead weights and that a ban on the use of lead would result in a sharp decline in lead poisoning.

Questions about Lead Poisoning

Since these findings, indicating that angling lead weights were having a serious impact on swans, were first published, we have been questioned closely about them. Here, we attempt to answer some of the most common questions.

(a) General Environmental Pollution

Some people suggest that the high lead levels in swans come from general lead pollution, from river boats, from lead in petrol, etc. This suggestion is false for a number of reasons. Firstly, birds living in the same area or piece of river, drinking the same water and eating the same foods, have very variable lead levels. If the lead came from the general environmental pollution, we should expect there to be much less variation. Even where the background levels of lead in the vegetation beside the river vary markedly between sites, the levels in the swans do not seem to be greatly affected by this: again suggesting that the background levels are not the root of the problem (J. Sears unpublished).

Secondly, in almost all the cases, high lead levels in the tissues are associated with the presence of lumps of lead in the gizzard, whereas birds dying of accidents virtually never have lead weights in their gizzards (Birkhead 1982). Such lumps of lead can hardly come from general pollution! Thirdly, the strong seasonal variation in lead levels in certain areas (Figure 7.1) cannot be reconciled with any known changes in environmental lead. Similar patterns are not found in unfished waters. Fourthly, for swans to accumulate as much lead as they do from river water (either directly, or indirectly via the aquatic vegetation) the water would have to contain so much lead that it would be dangerous to man. It should be remembered that the lead levels in most of our major rivers are closely monitored, as we drink the water ourselves.

Plate 22. Lead weights found in the gizzards of swans: the top row is gunshot, the middle row anglers' lead shot, and the third row anglers' split-shot after erosion in the gizzard. At the bottom is an anglers' ledger weight, also removed from a dead swan's gizzard. The penny piece shows the scale

(b) Much of the Lead Poisoning Blamed on Fishermen is actually Gunshot

This is not true. In England and Wales, fishing weights are responsible for the great majority of the deaths due to lead. On the River Thames, lead poisoning by gunshot has been found in only two out of 213 swans; in the MAFF sample, in only five out of 460; and in the ITE sample, in only six out of 392. Inland, those lead weights which can be identified in the birds are virtually all fishing weights. In some estuarine conditions, the proportion of swans dying from lead poisoning caused by gunshot is slightly higher, but it still remains a much less important cause of death than angling weights.

(c) Habitat Deterioration

Many anglers think that the continued deterioration of the habitat is responsible for the deaths of swans. Undoubtedly, there has been a loss of aquatic vegetation over the last 20 years or so, but at the same time most of our rivers have actually been cleaned up in a number of ways (Harrison and Grant 1976). Whatever the true position, it must be stressed that swans can, and do, live successfully for considerable periods on the rivers and then, suddenly, one will become sick and die; post-mortem reveals that it has died from having ingested anglers' lead weights. It is an inescapable fact that, however unsatisfactory the river may or may not be, the bird would have lived had it not been for the lead weights. This is not to say that there is no room for the improvement of our rivers, and indeed it is very worrying for both anglers and conservationists to note that river authorities all around the country are making serious cut-backs, especially in their monitoring and research divisions.

(d) Why Now?

One of the puzzles, and one often raised by anglers, concerns the suddenness of the decline in numbers of Mute Swans. How, anglers ask, can lead weights be responsible for the decline in swans when anglers have been using them for several hundred years without their apparently having any effect? There are three possible explanations why lead has only recently become a serious problem for Mute Swans:

(1) That the lost lead has been slowly building up in the environment over the years and is now present in such large quantities that the swans are almost bound to find it in their search for grit. Lead poisoning from the ingestion of gunshot is also more common in Scotland where there is little coarse fishing.

(2) That the amount of lead in the rivers has not changed that markedly, but that for some reason it is now easier for the swans to find it. One obvious way in which this would come about is that the wash from boats keeps silt from covering the discarded lead, so that it now remains exposed and available to swans for much longer than previously. Another suggestion is that, because the weed has gone, it is much easier for the swans to find the lead.

(3) That the amount of lead going into the environment each year has for some reason increased markedly.

We do not believe that the first two suggestions are likely to explain much of the change. If the first of these explanations is, however, correct, then the swans face a gloomy future because, even if the use of lead were totally withdrawn tomorrow, the birds would face poisoning for many years to come. There are two main reasons for thinking that this suggestion is wrong. First, there is, as we have shown, a strong seasonal pattern in the incidence of lead poisoning along the Thames, and it is difficult to see how this could happen if most of the lead poisoning were due to long-lost lead weights. Second, there is some evidence from the United States where lead gunshot has been banned because of the amount of poisoning to wildfowl and hunters have had to switch to non-toxic steel shot; within two years of the ban, about 50 per cent of the shot picked up by the birds was steel. This strongly suggests that the birds are most likely to find the more recently used shot; presumably, the shot slowly sinks into the ground so that that most recently fired is the most easily found.

Much the same objections can be applied to the second suggestion. It is difficult to see how the seasonal pattern of lead poisoning on the Thames could be explained by the effect of boats on the long-lost lead, either directly, or indirectly through the vegetation. It is true that there are more boats in the midsummer period, when lead poisoning is at its highest. The use of boats builds up steadily, however, during the spring and summer period, without a drop-off during the angling close season; since the latter is accompanied by a drop in the number of cases of lead poisoning, it is difficult to see how boating could be responsible.

As mentioned earlier in this chapter, we think that the evidence points to recently discarded lead weights as being the cause of the problem. If this is the case, we still need to explain why there was a large increase in the incidence of Mute Swan deaths from lead poisoning in the late 1950s/early 1960s. We believe that a major change in angling habits at that time may explain the sudden increase. Up to the mid-1950s, most anglers used cotton fishing lines. About the time in question, there was a progressive change from cotton to man-made fibres, initially nylon. These new lines were a very great improvement over the old ones, since they did not rot and did not need to be dried out and greased after a fishing trip. The use of these new lines heralded other changes to tackle which we think may have been important to our story. Anglers using the relatively thick and visible cotton lines used to tie their 'terminal tackle' to the end of the line. This consisted of a gut cast about 1m long, to which were attached the float, weights and, at one end, the hook; the latter was usually on a short, thinner cast of its own. At the end of the day, the cast, together with the float, weights and hook, was untied from the line and stored on a winder until the next fishing trip. With the advent of thin nylon lines, this habit changed. Nowadays, the hook, float and weights are attached directly to the line, and at the end of the day these are removed; the weights are just stripped from the line and, since they are awkward to open and re-use, are discarded. In spite of pleas to the contrary, many anglers, especially youngsters, just throw them away on site.

Two other aspects of this change over to nylon lines may, we think, be important. First, with the old system, if the hook snagged on something (even a swan!) and the angler pulled in his line and the tackle broke, the break usually occurred in the thinnest part, the short cast to which the hook was attached; the angler then successfully retrieved the rest of his tackle, including the lead weights. Nowadays, the end section is no more likely to break than the line higher up, since it is all of the same material. Indeed, the lead weights, tightly pinched onto the line, may well produce a point of weakness in the line, making it more likely to break at the weight; hence, at least some of the weights are likely to be lost as well as the hook. Finally, it is practicable to make these lines very much finer than the old cotton ones, and it has become the fashion to fish with very fine lines; these are much more likely to break if the hook is snagged. We believe therefore that the arrival of nylon mono-filament lines may have resulted in far higher quantities of lead entering the river, both when discarded after use and when lost while still attached to the lines. The advent of these habits was gradual, but the major changes occurred around the same time as the large increase in deaths of swans through lead poisoning. Although there is no conclusive proof, we believe that these changes in angling habits may have been the trigger for the changes in swan numbers.

Plate 23. Many swans get caught up in or swallow anglers' lost and discarded tackle. This swan swallowed a hook and its lead weights, only the float preventing the complete tackle from being ingested

The Amount of Lead Lost

The quantity of lead fishing weights lost each year is unknown. It is even hard to obtain records of how much lead is used in the manufacture of fishing weights each year. It has been suggested that one could consider that all the weights bought each year are purchased to replace those which are lost, though this would seem to be a slight exaggeration. Even so, the amount of lead actually sold by the angling trade does not seem to be known. Estimates run as high as 150 tons per year, though this figure certainly includes the very heavy sea-angling weights, and the proportion of it which goes to make the split-shot used on the fishing lines is unknown. More cautious estimates suggest that the amount might be nearer to 25 tons. Whatever the actual figure, it is clear that there are great quantities of shot distributed along the riverbanks. One has simply to go and look for it; it is only too easy to pick it up along the banks. In some areas, such as on concrete slipways, one can find great numbers of weights, as many as 1,961 per 120 square metres (J. Sears pers. comm.).

The most striking study of the rate at which lead weights get into the environment was undertaken by the University of Cardiff at Woodstock Pool in South Wales (Bell 1984). This is a small (1-ha), man-made pool which was not opened up for angling until 1978. Two fishing positions were investigated in detail in 1984, by removing the surface layer of soil from the bank and also the top few centimetres of the pool bottom for 2-2.5 m out from the bank. All this was meticulously searched for lead weights. A total of 1,451 weights weighing 504 g was found; this is equivalent to 27,000 weights weighing over 8 kg for the whole pool. A second study was carried out in 1984. At two of the angling 'pegs', plastic sheeting was spread over the ground, both on the bank and below the water line, and then covered with soil and gravel. This sheeting was left in position for 80 days of the fishing season, then gathered in and searched for lead weights. A total of 399 weights was found, equivalent to a loss rate of 2.5 per day per peg. It is perhaps worth noting that this is a well-managed angling site, and by 1984 there had been widespread publicity about the dangers of lead; the Angling Code, urging that anglers take the utmost care not to lose their weights, had also been widely circulated there.

The Number of Swans Dying from Lead Poisoning

The 1981 NCC report estimated that 3,000-3,500 Mute Swans died each year from lead poisoning. This estimate has come in for a great deal of criticism and certainly needs reconsideration. In the investigation, over England as a whole, 50 per cent of the swans died of lead poisoning (NCC 1981, Table 5, p. 17). At the time, it was thought that this might be biased towards the high side (the incidence of lead poisoning is sometimes higher in urban areas than in rural ones, so if more birds were sent in from urban areas than from rural ones this would lead to an over-estimate of the total number dying from lead poisoning). Because of this, and in order not to be thought to be trying to exaggerate the seriousness of the problem, a figure of 30 per cent of deaths caused by lead poisoning was used in the 1981 calculations.

The major problem is still to find what percentage of all swan deaths is due to lead poisoning. The extensive data from the East Anglian area do not suggest that there is much justification for using a figure of 30 per cent as the proportion dying from lead poisoning. It seems more reasonable to use the actual figures from the (now much more extensive) MAFF survey. For England, the figure has varied between years from 42.4 per cent to 58 per cent; the figure for the Thames study area, which includes both 'country' and 'town', is around 50 per cent. A calculation using these figures would suggest that something between 2,220 and 3,040 fully grown Mute Swans are dying each year from lead poisoning.

To this needs to be added the number of cygnets that die of lead poisoning. Since this stage is the one where natural mortality is highest, it may not be reasonable to apply the same death rates from lead poisoning to this age group. Nevertheless, in some areas, mortality of cygnets from lead is very high. Once again, a conservative estimate — of 25 per cent — was used; this gives 1,150 cygnets dying from lead poisoning. Hence, this recalculation would suggest that of the order of 3,370 to 4,190 swans die in England each year from ingesting fishing weights; to this can be added a small number from Scotland and Wales, from where the data are rather too sparse to make any calculation.

This estimate is slightly higher than the previous one largely because the more extensive number of post-mortems suggest that a higher death rate should be used in the calculations. Some care needs to be exercised in the use of these figures. They should be taken to imply that the situation still remains extremely serious and probably *unchanged* since the previous estimate. They should *not* be taken as evidence of an increase in the incidence of lead poisoning, but rather as showing that the previous estimate was probably over-cautious.

Substitutes for Lead

With the publication of the Nature Conservancy Council Report (1981), anglers were put under considerable pressure to stop using lead. Equally, manufacturers were encouraged to try to find suitable substitutes for lead.

This was easier said than done. Anglers have two main requirements from the material with which they weight their lines. It must be as dense and small as possible so as not to be too conspicuous to the fish, and it must be soft enough to be shaped because they need to be able to pinch the weights onto the line. Lead is the ideal substance from both points of view, and no other readily available material has these specifications – except gold!

There was no shortage of ideas, but there was a considerable delay before actual substances were produced for anglers to try out. Many anglers found the early substitutes for lead difficult to use, and some objected to them on the grounds that they were more expensive than lead. The former objection was not unreasonable with regard to some of the earlier versions, as they were not ideal fishing weights, but the latter was more difficult to sustain. Since all the substitutes are designed to be re-usable, it is not relevant simply to compare the prices with that of lead; a more expensive, but re-usable, material should be cheaper in the long run than an initially cheaper, but disposable, substance.

By late 1984, there were several substances available on the market, although they were not selling very well. By the middle of the following year, two of the leading angling bodies had accepted that two of the substitutes were, if properly used, adequate replacements for lead.

At this stage, the Minister for the Environment announced that lead must be withdrawn from use. While the Minister hoped that this could be done voluntarily by the anglers themselves, draft legislation was being prepared to ban its use by early 1987 and this legislation would be brought into action through the regional water authorities if it was felt necessary.

We feel that a ban will be necessary. Already many anglers have accepted that lead is causing serious problems for Mute Swans and that they should stop using it. Nevertheless, even if all the serious anglers were to stop using lead tomorrow, there are enormous numbers of children and casual anglers who have nothing to do with any of the angling organisations; the high incidence of lead poisoning in summer suggests that it is these groups who may be a major part of the problem. Unless they can be reached by some sort of ban on the use of lead, the efforts of other anglers are unlikely to prove effective. If such a ban can be introduced, the future for swans would seem rosier.

CHAPTER

8

The Future

We cannot really leave the subject of our Mute Swans without considering what the future holds for them in Britain. They live in a habitat that is much in demand; it provides our water supplies and is used for recreation of many sorts. In addition to the water itself, the swans need access to the riverside; at least at times, they need to get out on to the bank, either for feeding or for nesting.

Since the swans now live in such a managed part of our environment, it is inevitable that much of what we do to that environment will affect them also. Can we foresee what the future holds?

In recent years, and at the present, the swans have been having a very bad time. As we have explained, a high proportion of their current problems stem from lead poisoning. There seems every reason to hope that, if the use of this poisonous substance can be phased out, swans will be relieved of a major problem which not only must have contributed to their decline over a wide area of England, but which also, for many individuals, results in a lingering and unpleasant death. Although a few anglers still believe that the decline in numbers in the swan population cannot be blamed on lead, there is no doubt that the deaths of many individuals are the result of their picking up lead fishing weights.

Although the swallowing of lead weights is the main cause of death of swans in many areas, the RSPCA and the swan rescue services are all too frequently called out because swans are entangled in hooks and lines. This issue will not go away if lead is banned, and education of at least certain groups of anglers will still be necessary if this problem is to be reduced.

Looking at the brighter side of things, if the use of substitutes for lead can be arranged, there seems every reason to suppose that the situation will rapidly improve, since, as we have already explained, we believe that many swans die from swallowing lead weights that have been recently lost or discarded. If a high proportion of the birds that die of lead poisoning do so because they have picked up long-discarded weights, then any improvement — resulting from the use of substitutes — will be slower.

In most areas, breeding adults are less susceptible to lead poisoning than the younger birds. In such places, an increase in breeding numbers will take a few years to come into effect since it can come about only through an improvement in the survival of the young birds, and these will take time to filter through into the breeding population. Improvement in breeding numbers could be more rapid in places, such as perhaps the Lower Thames, where not just the survival of the young but also that of the adults is poor; if the survival rates of these adults were to increase as a result of withdrawal of lead, breeding numbers could increase quite rapidly.

If we can get rid of lead, the Mute Swan population should start to rise again. A few words of caution, however, are needed. From time to time, we meet some rather oversimplified views about the population dynamics of the Mute Swan. One of these is that, if the use of lead fishing weights were to cease, all the birds that are currently dying of lead poisoning would then survive and so the population would rise at a very rapid rate. This is rather optimistic for two reasons. First, a percentage of the swans that die each year do so from other causes; presumably, a proportion of those birds that formerly would have died of lead poisoning would now die from these other causes. To take an oversimplified example: suppose that a population of swans produced 200 cygnets each year of which 100 (50 per cent) died from lead poisoning in the summer and another 50 (50 per cent of the remainder) from flying into wires in the winter, leaving only 50 survivors; if one removed lead as a hazard, one might hope to find that there were an extra 100 birds surviving, since all those that had formerly died of lead poisoning would now survive. It is, however, more likely that there would be only 100 birds alive at the end of the year (50 per cent of 200), not 150, since more of the birds would now die from flying into wires. As we have said, this is oversimplified, but it does indicate one of the problems of estimating the likely changes in numbers when there are environmental changes.

The second error is to assume that all deaths are independent of each other. Birds interact with one another: they compete for limited resources. As any population rises, competition between individuals becomes more severe and so, progressively, more of the birds will lose out as a result of competition with their fellows. In particular, if the population of Mute Swans were to rise to its previous levels, severe competition for breeding sites might occur, with the result that some birds would be forced to remain longer in the non-breeding flocks before they could obtain a territory; this would be much the same situation as that at the end of the 1950s.

Plate 24. It is unlikely that the Mute Swan will ever reach its former abundance of the 1950s. These swans were caught for ringing at Abbotsbury in Dorset when they were flightless

How Many Swans Should There Be?

Assuming that the numbers do increase again, do we need to consider how many swans there should be? We have said that we do not know how many Mute Swans there were in a 'natural' Britain, but in any case the question itself is barely relevant. Lowland Britain has been changed so much since man first arrived on the scene, and the history of the Mute Swan since then has been anything but natural. It is hardly surprising that many natural forms of regulation no longer affect the numbers of Mute Swans. Wolves and bears no longer take their toll; the winter food supply, which may once have imposed serious limitations, is very different now. Nowadays, it is man's activities that seem to set the limits on swan numbers. Perhaps the time has come to plan more carefully for the future. If so, what criteria can we use to formulate our plans?

Almost everyone would agree that swans are now scarcer than is desirable; a mere 30 or so pairs on the Thames between London and Oxford is a poor number by almost any standards, and many other rivers are in at least as poor a state. If the swans should start to increase again, however, we will have to realise two things: we may have to consider caring for them in winter, and we may have to find ways of limiting their numbers on good farmland.

The swans are often locally short of food in late winter and they sometimes turn to farmers' fields for food. With greatly diminished opportunities for swans to graze other than on expensively 'improved' grasslands, any increase in their number is likely to be accompanied by complaints about them. At present, swans cause only a minor amount of damage on farms. In a field or two here and there it may be serious, but on a national scale it is so small that it can hardly count at all (page 119); indeed, currently, there are only some 12, very localised, areas where people have suggested that Mute Swans may be a problem to farmers. If the numbers of swans increase, complaints about agricultural damage may become more common and, even though they are never likely to become serious on a national scale, we may need to think about what should be done about such damage. Some of the birds already congregate on reserves, and many of the swans in non-breeding flocks get much of their food from the public. Will the public continue to provide enough food? Even if they are not prepared to do so, they will almost certainly complain if they think the birds are starving. Consideration may have to be given to providing the birds with more refuges where they can feed safely in the winter. Large flocks of non-breeders in towns have probably always put a strain on the natural resources, and nowadays that strain may be more serious unless the situation is properly organised.

Let us suppose that the current moves to phase out the use of lead angling weights are successful and that the numbers of Mute Swans increase until they reach the levels of the 1920s and 1930s. What would we do about it? How do we decide, on objective, scientific grounds, what is an acceptable number? The reductions attempted before the war were undertaken against a background of burgeoning numbers, but, so far as we can discover, no-one seems to have had any very clear idea of what level of swan numbers they were aiming to achieve. One thing is certain: there is little likelihood of getting everyone to agree! Even supposing there were general agreement that Mute Swans were becoming too numerous, it is difficult to see what would be the best thing to do about it. Today, culls would be illegal without a licence, and one would be granted only if the swans could be clearly shown to be doing damage and that alternative methods to prevent the damage would not be effective. Whatever the problem, it seems hardly likely that culls of fully grown birds in winter, as were conducted in the 1930s, would be acceptable today.

If numbers were to be reduced, the only acceptable way might be to undertake wide-scale egg-removal. This is also illegal without a licence, and in any case it might well not have the desired effect: there are both theoretical and practical difficulties. First, the taking of eggs is a slow and difficult way to control a population, since the birds that hatched from those eggs would anyway not have bred for a further four years or so. Second, the removal would have to be extremely thorough to have much effect. If some 20 per cent of the nests were missed, the effect of egg-removal could be very slight; lack of competition would allow the cygnets from these nests to flourish. Egg-removal is therefore a difficult and time-consuming operation which must be maintained for many years if it is to be effective. In addition, one can envisage strong local opposition to it. It is one thing to agree that there may be too many swans, but quite another to accept that most of the eggs should be taken from the only nest on one's property!

Other Management Problems

Even if there is an increase in the Mute Swan population as a result of the withdrawal of lead fishing weights, it is by no means certain that the swans will return to their earlier numbers. Although lead poisoning is a very serious problem for the swans, and one would expect some sort of increase if the problem were removed, numbers may well not reach their former levels. The situation on the River Thames is markedly different from what it was 20 to 30 years ago and the number of swans that can be accommodated on the river may well be lower than it used to be. Several features are less favourable for swans now than they were previously. There is, for example, clearly much less aquatic vegetation than there once was. This may well be a result of increased traffic of boats, which both mechanically (with their wash) damage or remove the plants and, by churning up the water, make it more turbid and so prevent light from reaching plants below the surface, resulting in poorer growth. Many anglers maintain that the condition of the river has deteriorated markedly as a result of heavy boat traffic. There is also considerable and growing concern about the long-term effects of the run-off of large quantities of agricultural chemicals, both fertilisers and pesticides, into the rivers.

At least as important to the swans is what has happened to the riverside. In many places, the wash of boats has eroded the banks and made them too steep for the swans to get out easily, although in most areas they can still find spots where they can do so. At a pinch they can fly out if they need to, though they cannot do this with small cygnets or when they are in moult. Worse still, when they do get out, the grass which they need to graze has disappeared from many areas, resulting in a shortage of food for them. This is not yet serious on the upper reaches of the Thames or on the smaller rivers, but on many stretches of the Lower Thames food is becoming decidedly hard to find.

In addition, safe nesting sites are becoming progressively scarcer, and this is a problem for many species of waterbirds, not just the swans. One reason for this has been the increasing steepness of the banks in many places; these are not the sorts of waterside where one finds good stands of aquatic vegetation. Once again, the wash of boats must largely take the blame.

Canada Geese are now so successful on our lowland rivers that they may soon become a serious problem

Another problem has been identified, although no-one at present knows how serious it may be or may become. The increasing numbers of Canada Geese, *Branta canadensis*, may, in some areas, make life difficult for swans. There seem to be no problems where there are just one or two pairs of geese; the swans, which are much larger, can easily see them off. Pairs of geese and swans may nest successfully within a few metres of each other on an island. Nevertheless, there are anecdotal records of areas, mostly small lakes, where swans used to nest but now do not, and which have in the interval been taken over by large flocks of geese. Is the disappearance of the swans just part of the widespread decline or have they left, as is suggested, because of the geese? Cause and effect have not been convincingly established, and certainly there are many stretches of river which are nowadays without Mute Swans, but which do not yet hold Canada Geese in any numbers. Nevertheless, the goose population is still increasing steadily, at perhaps as much as 8 per cent per annum (Ogilvie 1977). Flocks of 400 or more can be seen along the Thames in summer. The geese's feeding habits — largely grazing away from the water — do not seem to result in their picking up many lead fishing weights, though in the United States many have died from ingesting gunshot. Even if they are not a major problem for the swans, the Canada Geese seem likely to become one for someone in the not far distant future!

Habitat Management

So, the future still holds many problems for the Mute Swans, but most of these are not beyond our abilities to cope with if only we have the determination to do so. In many areas, some of their problems with the habitat could be overcome to some extent by a little careful planning. Wherever there are islands, it ought to be possible to provide safe nesting sites. It should be possible to limit the damage done by boats by restricting their passage to one side of the islands: something which happens in some areas anyway. It should then be possible to maintain gentle slopes and good riverside vegetation on the side away from the boat traffic.

Finding ways of improving the riverside aquatic vegetation is something which would not benefit merely the swans, but also other wildlife, including fish. Most problems with the riverside vegetation seem to arise from the boat traffic, and attempts to find ways of limiting wave action and turbulence are being made, but not yet on a scale large enough to have any practical effect.

Shortage of nesting sites is also becoming more widespread on the small, unnavigated rivers, though for a different reason. Here, farmers have progressively removed the riverside vegetation, either because they now grow crops up to the river edge or because they allow their cattle to graze up to the water's edge. The problems created by this are compounded by the action of many Water Authorities in their dredging operations. Dredging of many of these small rivers is inevitably necessary from time to time. The way in which it is done, however, is, perhaps for reasons of economy, very unimaginative from the point of view of wildlife. There is a tendency to make these small rivers straighter and steeper-sided, so that they become progressively more canal-like. It is the shallow, floodable verges and the river bends that are so important to wildlife. No self-respecting swan is going to struggle up a vertical bank and nest in an open field. Some Water Authorities are now trying to see whether they can find ways of managing these small rivers more imaginatively without greatly increasing the cost. Here again, there is urgent need for such experiments to become more widespread. An obvious way of improving conditions would be to cut channels so as to leave islands where the birds can safely nest. This is not very difficult on even the smallest streams; normally, the downstream end of an island will naturally alter to form a gentle slope into the water, allowing easy access, and aquatic vegetation will flourish in the shallows there. In many areas, the small rivers are still attractive havens for wildlife, but in some areas management operations have resulted in their becoming seriously degraded.

In short, we should like to see the river system improved, especially with efforts made to increase the plantlife both on the banks and in the streams. Such changes would not merely benefit the swans, but would also benefit the fish, the other wildlife, and ultimately the river as an amenity for ourselves. We should not forget that the rivers are our own life-blood, since we rely on them for drinking water. There is every reason why we should want to see a healthy river system regardless of the swans.

Many of these things that need to be done are neither particularly difficult nor expensive; they need just imaginative management. They will be of benefit to almost everyone, as well as to the subject of this book. We cannot improve on Yarrell's view that

'The swan is, perhaps, of all the others, the most beautiful living ornament of our lakes and rivers.'

Bibliography

Amman, G.A. 1937. Number of contour feathers in *Cygnus* and *Xanthocephalus. Auk* 54:201-2.

Andersen-Harild, P. 1978. *The Mute Swan.* Copenhagen Skarv. Nature publications [in Danish].

Bacon, P.E. 1980a. Status and dynamics of a Mute Swan population near Oxford between 1976 and 1978. *Wildfowl* 31:37-50.

—— 1980b. A possible advantage of the 'Polish' morph of the Mute Swan. *Wildfowl* 31:51-2.

Banko, W.E. 1962. Economic Uses of Swans in Russia. *Atlantic Nat.* 17:109-10, 130.

Bell, D. 1984. The Impact of Anglers on Wildlife and Site Amenity. Pub. Dept of Applied Biology, Institute of Science and Technology, University of Wales, Cardiff.

Berglund, B.E., Curry-Lindahl, K., Luther, H., Olsson, V., Rodhe, W., and Sellerberg, G. 1963. Ecological studies on the Mute Swan (*Cygnus olor*) in south-eastern Sweden. *Acta Vertebratica* 2:163-288.

Birkhead, M.E. 1982a. Population Ecology and Lead Poisoning in the Mute Swan. D.Phil Thesis, Oxford University.

—— 1982b. Causes of mortality in the Mute Swan. *J. Zool.* 198:1-11.

—— 1983. Lead levels in the blood of Mute Swans. *J. Zool.* 199:59-73.

—— 1984. Variation in the weight and composition of Mute Swan eggs. *Condor* 86:489-90.

—— Bacon, P.J., and Walter, P. 1983. Factors affecting the breeding success of the Mute Swan. *J. Anim. Ecol.* 52:727-41.

—— and Perrins, C.M. 1985. The breeding biology of the Mute Swan on the river Thames with special reference to lead poisoning. *Biol. Cons.* 31:1-11.

Bloch, D. 1970. [The Mute Swan *Cygnus olor* breeding in a colony in Denmark]. *Dansk. Orn. Foren. Tidssk.* 64:152-62 [in Danish, with English summary].

Blurton Jones, N.G. 1956. Census of breeding Canada Geese 1953. *Bird Study* 3:153-70.

Boase, H. 1959. Notes on the display, nesting and moult of the Mute Swan. *Brit. Birds* 52:114-23.

Boyd, H., and Ogilvie, M.A. 1964. Losses of Mute Swans in England in the winter 1962-63. *Wildfowl Trust Ann. Rep.* 15:37-40.

Brenneke, H-E. 1962. Zur Ausbreitung des Höckerschwans und zur Frage seiner Fischereischadlichkeit. *Orn. Mitt.* 14:171-2.

Brown, A.W., and Brown, L.M. 1984. The status of Mute Swans in the Lothians. *Scot. Birds* 13:8-15.

—— and —— 1985. The Scottish Mute Swan census. *Scot. Birds* 13:140-8.

Bruun, B. 1960. [Distribution of the Mute Swan (*Cygnus olor* (Gm)) at the coast and in the interior of Denmark 1935-59]. *Dansk. Orn. Foren. Tidssk.* 54:77-84 [in Danish, with English summary].

Campbell, B. 1960. The Mute Swan Census in England and Wales 1955-56. *Bird Study* 7:208-23.

Church, H.F. 1956. The Mute Swan population of the eastern borders. *Bird Study* 3:212-17.

Clarke, E.G., and Clarke, M.L. 1975. *Veterinary Toxicology.* 3rd ed. Baillière, London.

Coleman, A.E., and Minton, C.D.T. 1979. Pairing and breeding of Mute Swans in relation to natal area. *Wildfowl* 30:27-30.

—— and —— 1980. Mortality of Mute Swan progeny in an area of south Staffordshire. *Wildfowl* 31:22-8.

Collins, R. 1985. Movement of a Mute Swan from Ireland to Britain. *Irish Birds* 3:98-9.

Cook, R.S., and Trainer, D.O. 1966. Experimental lead poisoning of Canada Geese. *J. Wildl. Mgt* 30:1-8.

Cramp, S. 1957. A report on the census of Mute Swans, 1955 and 1956. *London Bird Report* 56:58-62.

—— and Simmons, K.E.L. (eds.) 1977. *The Birds of the Western Palearctic,* Vol. I. Oxford University Press.

Cross, A. 1947. Display of the Mute Swan. *Brit. Birds.* 40:279.

Dementiev, G.P., and Gladkov, N.A. 1951-52. *Birds of the USSR.* Vol 4. Moscow [in Russian].

Dewar, J.M. 1942. The Mute Swan and the 20-10 seconds rule. *Brit. Birds* 35:225-6.

Eltringham, S.K. 1963a. The British population of the Mute Swan. *Bird Study* 10:10-28.

—— 1963b. Is the Mute Swan a menace? *Bird Notes* 30:285-9.

—— 1966. The survival of Mute Swan cygnets. *Bird Study* 13:204-7.

French, M.C. In prep. Causes of mortality of the Mute Swan in East Anglia.

Gillham, M.E. 1956. Feeding habits and seasonal movements of Mute Swans in south Devon estuaries. *Bird Study* 3:205-12.

Goethe, F. 1965. Weissfische als Trabanten des Höckerschwans. *Natur. Mus.* 95:116-17.

Hardman, J.A., and Cooper, D.R. 1980. Mute Swans on the Warwickshire Avon — a study of a decline. *Wildfowl* 31:29-36.

Harle, D. 1951. Mute Swans feeding on standing oats. *Brit. Birds* 44:287-8.

Harrison, J.G. 1963. Heavy mortality of Mute Swans from electrocution. *Wildfowl Trust Ann. Rep.* 14:164-5.

— and Grant, P. 1976. *The Thames Transformed*. Andre Deutsch, London.

— and Ogilvie, M.A. 1967. Immigrant Mute Swans in south-east England. *Wildfowl Trust Ann. Rep.* 18:85-7.

Harting, J.E. 1895. On the origin of the terms 'cob' and 'pen'. *Zoologist* 19:372-4.

— 1896. Strength of wing in the swan. *Zoologist* 20:356.

Harwood, M. 1982. Unmiraculous comeback of the Trumpeter Swan. *Audubon Mag.* 84:32-43.

Heinroth, O. 1911. Beiträge zur Biologie, namentlich Ethologie und Psychologie der Anatiden. *Proc. Int. Orn. Congr. Berlin* 5:598-702.

— and Heinroth, M. 1924-28. *Die Vögel Mitteleuropas.* Vol 3. Berlin.

Hilprecht, A. 1970. *Höckerschwan, Singschwan, Zwergschwan.* Neue Brehm-Bücherei, Wittenberg.

Howard, W.J.H. 1935. Notes on the nesting of captive Mute Swans. *Wilson Bull.* 47:237-8.

Hulme, D.C. 1948. Mute Swan eating dead fish. *Brit. Birds* 41:121.

Hunt, J. 1815. *British Ornithology.* Vol 2. Bacon, Norwich.

Hunt, A.E. 1980. Mute Swan investigations — lead poisoning. *BTO News* 110:1-2.

Hutton, M. 1980. Metal contamination of feral pigeons *Columba livia* from the London area: part 2 — biological effects of lead exposure. *Environ. Pollution* (A) 22:281-93.

Huxley, J.S. 1947. Display of the Mute Swan. *Brit. Birds* 40:130-4.

Jenkins, D., Newton, I., and Brown, C. 1976. Structure and dynamics of a Mute Swan population. *Wildfowl* 27:77-82.

Jensen, F. 1967. [The Mute Swan (*Cygnus olor*) breeding at Bognes]. *Dansk. Orn. Foren. Tidssk.* 61:143-50 [in Danish, with English summary].

Jogi, A., Lipsberg, J., and Nedzinskas, V. 1974. Numbers and seasonal distribution of the East Baltic population of the Mute Swan. In Kumari, E. (ed.), Material of the Conference on the study and conservation of migratory birds in the Baltic Basin. Acad. Sci. Estonian S.S.R. Tallinn.

Johnsgard, P.A. 1965. *Handbook of Waterfowl Behaviour.* Cornell Univ. Press, Ithaca.

Kear, J. 1964. Colour preference in young Anatidae. *Ibis* 106: 361-9.

— 1965. The internal food reserves of hatching Mallard ducklings. *J. Wildl. Manag.* 29:523-8.

Kennedy, P.G., Ruttledge, R.F., and Scroope, C.F. 1954. *The Birds of Ireland.* Oliver and Boyd, London.

Kumari, E. (ed.) 1970. *Waterfowl in Estonia.* Valgus Publ., Tallinn.

Lack, D. 1968. The proportion of yolk in the eggs of waterfowl. *Wildfowl* 19:67-9.

Lessells, C.M. 1976. Unpublished Honours project, Oxford University.

Ling, P.G. 1961. On new colonies of *Cygnus olor* in the Estonian SSR. *Acad. Nauk Latviisk SSR:* 81-3.

Lloyd, L. 1854. *Scandinavian adventures during a residence of upwards of twenty years.* Vol. 2, pp. 431-50. Publ. for the Surtees Soc. by G. Andrews, Durham.

Lockwood, W.B. 1984. *The Oxford Book of British Bird Names.* Oxford University Press.

Low, G.C. 1935. The extent to which captivity modifies the habits of birds. *Bull. BOC.* 55:144-54.

Luther, H. 1963. Ecological studies on the Mute Swan. IX. Botanical analysis of Mute Swan faeces. *Acta Vertebratica* 2:265-7.

MacLeod, R.D. 1954. *Key to the names of British Birds.* Pitman, London.

MacSwiney of Mashanaglas, M. 1971. *Six Came Flying.* Michael Joseph, London.

Mathiasson, S. 1973. A moulting population of non-breeding Mute Swans with special reference to flight feather moult, feeding ecology and habitat selection. *Wildfowl* 24:43-53.

May, D.J. 1947. Notes on the winter territory of a pair of Mute Swans. *Brit. Birds* 40:326-7.

Mayaud, N. 1962. A propos de la réproduction en France du Cygne tuberculé *Cygnus olor. Alauda* 30:148-50.

Minton, C.D.T. 1968. Pairing and breeding of Mute Swans. *Wildfowl* 19:41-60.

—— 1971. Mute Swan flocks. *Wildfowl* 22:71-88.

Mudge, G.P. 1983. The incidence and significance of ingested lead pellet poisoning in British Wildfowl. *Biol. Conserv.* 27:333-72.

Munro, R.E., Smith, L.T., and Kupa, J.J. 1968. The genetic basis of colour differences observed in the Mute Swan (*Cygnus olor*). *Auk* 85:504-5.

Nature Conservancy Council. 1981. Lead Poisoning in Swans. Report of the Nature Conservancy Council's Working Group.

Naumann, J.A., and Naumann, J.F. 1905. Naturgeschichte der Vögel Deutschlands.

Ogilvie, M.A. 1967. Population changes and mortality of the Mute Swan in Britain. *Wildfowl Trust Ann. Rep.* 18:64-73.

—— 1972. Distribution, numbers and migration. Pp. 29-55 in Scott, P., and the Wildfowl Trust, 1972.

—— 1977. The numbers of Canada Geese in Britain, 1976. *Wildfowl* 28:27-34.

—— 1981. The Mute Swan in Britain, 1978. *Bird Study* 28:87-106.

Ogilvie, M.A. 1986. The Mute Swan in Britain, 1983. *Bird Study* (in press).

O'Halloran, J., and Duggan, P.F. 1984. Lead levels in Mute Swans in Cork. *Irish Birds* 2:501-14.

Olsson, V. 1963. Ecological studies on the Mute Swan. VIII. Nutritional biology of the Mute Swan in Valdemarsviken in Småland and Östergötland. *Acta Vertebratica* 2:256-64.

—— 1964. [Some changes in the bird fauna of the Swedish East Coast]. *Vår Fågelvärld* 23:352-62 [in Swedish, with English summary].

Owen, M., and Cadbury C.J. 1975. The ecology and mortality of Swans on the Ouse Washes, England. *Wildfowl* 16:31-42.

Parkin, D.T., and McMeeking, J.M. 1985. The increase of Canada Geese in Nottinghamshire from 1980. *Bird Study* 32:132-40.

Patrick, R.W. 1935. Mute Swan attacking bullock. *Brit. Birds* 29:116.

Perrins, C.M. 1981. Mortality of Mute Swans. Unpublished report to the NCC working party on Lead Poisoning in Swans.

— and Ogilvie, M.A. 1981. A study of the Abbotsbury Mute Swans. *Wildfowl* 32:35-47.

— and Reynolds, C.M. 1967. A preliminary study of the Mute Swan, *Cygnus olor. Wildfowl Trust Ann. Rep.* 18:74-84.

Phillips, J.C. 1928. Wild birds introduced or transplanted in North America. Tech. Bull. No. 61. U.S. Dept Agric.

— and Lincoln, F.C. 1930. *American Waterfowl.* Houghton Mifflin, Boston and New York.

Plot, R. 1686. *The Natural History of Staffordshire.* Oxford.

Portielje, A.F.J. 1936. Ein bemerkenswerter Grenzfall von Polygamie bzw. accessorischer Promiskuität beim Höckerschwan, zugleich ein Beitrag zur Ethologie bzw. Psychologie von *Cygnus olor. J. Orn.* 84:140-58.

Rawcliffe, C.P. 1958. The Scottish Mute Swan census 1955-56. *Bird Study* 5:45-55

Reynolds, C.M. 1965. The survival of Mute Swan cygnets. *Bird Study* 12:128-9.

— 1971. The Mute Swans of the Oxford area. *Proc. Symp. IWRB,* Slimbridge.

— 1972. Mute Swan weights in relation to breeding performance. *Wildfowl* 23:111-18.

Roscoe, D.E. 1978. Pathology and Plumbism in waterfowl and development of a simple diagnostic blood test. PhD thesis, Univ. of Connecticut.

Royal Commission on Environmental Pollution. 1983. *Ninth report: Lead in the environment.* HMSO, London.

Salmon, D.G. 1985. Number of swans and ducks in Britain, 1983-84. *Wildfowl* 36:151.

Sebastiano, R. and Delprato, P. 1880. *Degli uccelli domestici e semidomestici L'Ornipogyapria o la Medicina,* Pisa:433-7.

Scott, D.K. 1984. Winter territoriality of Mute Swans *Cygnus olor. Ibis* 126:168-76.

—— 1984. Parent-offspring association in Mute Swans. *Zeit. für Tierpsychol.* 64:74-86.

— and Birkhead, M.E. 1983. Resources and reproductive performance in Mute Swans. *J. Zool.* 200:539-47.

Scott, P., and The Wildfowl Trust. 1972. *The Swans.* Michael Joseph, London.

Seegar, W.S. 1979. Prevalence of parasitic heartworm in swans in England. *Wildfowl* 30:147-50.

Simpson, V.O., Hunt, A.E., and French, M.C. 1979. Chronic lead poisoning in a herd of Mute Swans. *Environ. Pollution* 18:187-202.

Sokolowski, J. 1960. *The Mute Swan in Poland.* State Council for Conservation of Nature, Warsaw.

Spärck, R. 1957. An investigation of the food of swans and ducks in Denmark. *Trans. Congr. Int. Union Game Biol.* 3:45-7.

Spray, C. 1981. Movements of Mute Swans from Scotland to Ireland. *Irish Birds* 2:82-4.

—— 1981. An isolated population of *Cygnus olor* in Scotland. Proc. 2nd Intern. Swan Symposium, Sapporo, Japan. (Publ. by Intern. Wildfowl Res. Bureau, Slimbridge, England.)

Stevenson, H. 1890. *The Birds of Norfolk.* Vol. 3, pp. 58-121. Gurney and Jackson, London.

Terras-Wahlberg, N. 1960. Knölsvanen (*Cygnus olor*) i Närke år 1957. *Vår Fågelvärld* 19:227-35.

Thomas, G.J. 1975. Ingested lead pellets in waterfowl at the Ouse Washes, England, 1968-1973.

—— 1980. A review of ingested lead poisoning in wildfowl. *Int. Waterfowl Res. Bull.* 46:43-60.

Ticehurst, N.F. 1895. On the origin of the terms 'Cob' and 'Pen'. *Zoologist* 1895:372-4.

—— 1941. The Mute Swan on the River Thames. *South-eastern Naturalist for 1941*:53-6.

—— 1957. *The Mute Swan in England.* Cleaver Hume.

Van IJzendoorn, A.L.J. 1951. The Mute Swan in Holland. *Audubon* 53:164-72.

Winge, A. 1959. Knölsvanen (*Cygnus olor*) i Skåne år 1957. *Vår Fågelvärld* 18:1-11 [in Swedish, with English summary].

Yarrell, W. 1838. (On the naming of *Cygnus immutabilis*). *Proc. Zool. Soc. for 1838*:19.

—— 1841. On a new species of swan (*Cygnus immutabilis*). *Proc. Zool. Soc.* 9:70.

—— 1845. *A History of British Birds.* Vol. 3. Van Doorst, London.

Index

To Nancy and Bob Birkhead
and
To Mary Perrins

THE MUTE SWAN